DESIGNING
SCHOOLS AND SCHOOLING
FOR THE HANDICAPPED

DESIGNING
SCHOOLS AND SCHOOLING
FOR THE HANDICAPPED

**A Guide to the Dynamic Interaction
of Space, Instructional Materials, Facilities,
Educational Objectives and Teaching Methods.**

By

JACK W. BIRCH, Ph.D.
*Professor, School of Education
University of Pittsburgh*

and

B. KENNETH JOHNSTONE, F.A.I.A.
*Johnstone, Newcomer & Valentour
Architects*

CHARLES C THOMAS · PUBLISHER
Springfield · Illinois · U.S.A.

Published and Distributed Throughout the World by
CHARLES C THOMAS · PUBLISHER
BANNERSTONE HOUSE
301-327 East Lawrence Avenue, Springfield, Illinois, U.S.A.

© 1975, by CHARLES C THOMAS · PUBLISHER
ISBN 0-398-03362-5
Library of Congress Catalog Card Number: 74-23213

With THOMAS BOOKS *careful attention is given to all details of manufacturing and design. It is the Publisher's desire to present books that are satisfactory as to their physical qualities and artistic possibilities and appropriate for their particular use.* THOMAS BOOKS *will be true to those laws of quality that assure a good name and good will.*

Printed in the United States of America
00-19

Library of Congress Cataloging in Publication Data

Birch, Jack W.
    Designing schools and schooling for the handicapped.
    Bibliography: p.
    Includes index.

    1. School buildings. 2. Handicapped children—Education. I. Johnstone, Burton Kenneth, 1907-   joint author. II. Title. [DNLM: 1. Architecture. 2. Facility design and construction. 3. Handicapped. 4. Schools. LB3325.H3 B617d]
LB3209.B46   371.9'045   74-23213
ISBN 0-398-03362-5

Dedication
To Jane and Helene

PREFACE

THIS BOOK IS a first attempt to establish guidelines for planning and designing teaching space and related services to maximize the education of children who are handicapped by body impairment, by mental, emotional or social dysfunction, or learning disability. The areas of exceptionality include the problems of (a) limited motor systems, (b) hearing impairment, (c) sight impairment, (d) limited communications systems, (e) mental retardation, (f) neurological impairment, (g) emotional disturbance, (h) social maladjustment, and (i) other educationally limiting conditions including multiple handicaps.

The book emphasizes the rapidly growing trend to accommodate more and more handicapped children in regular classrooms and resource rooms in the nation's elementary and secondary schools. Significant attention is also paid to special schools required by those handicapped pupils who cannot manage in the mainstream of education.

The material should apply to the design of new space or to the remodeling of existing space. Guidelines are offered for the inclusion of handicapped children in the regular school, including both the self-contained classroom type and the contemporary open plan, as well as for the optimum development of handicapped children in separate schools, where that is appropriate.

Design teams in the past have overlooked or ignored the needs of exceptional pupils. In a few instances, buildings make minor concessions to their needs, such as sections "adjusted for handicapped pupils." But designing to make schools in general good places for handicapped persons has not been the rule.

Local special education administrators are known to be inhibited from operating with optimum effectiveness because of shortcomings in present facilities. They are constrained by outmoded facilities and insufficient equipment for the special education programs, and that is especially true of resource rooms.

Each year a group of architects from the American Institute of Architects and a group of educators from the American Association of School Administrators are named to a jury to study school buildings submitted to the AASA Exhibition of School Architecture. "The purpose of jury citations granted to selected projects in the exhibition has been to call attention to outstanding features of individual projects."

As is indicated in the annual announcement of the exhibit, these criteria are used:

> In selecting entries for the exhibition, the jury will give prime consideration to the architectural solution of the stated educational program requirements. Plans should be uniquely adapted to the educational program and should clearly reflect the challenge presented to the architect and how this challenge was met. Specifically, the jury will give consideration to the following:
>
> | | |
> |---|---|
> | Adequacy for educational program | Environmental controls: |
> | Aesthetics | light, air, sound |
> | Grouping of instructional areas | Safety |
> | Accessibility of facilities | Adaptation to site |
> | Flexibility—expansibility | Site development |
> | Community use | Presentation of materials |

The accepted plans and descriptions are displayed nationally. The 1974 exhibition included 232 projects. Forty were selected for citations and two for awards. Of that group seven were special schools for handicapped children, and a number of others were regular schools designed to include handicapped children.

We believe the joint AASA-AIA appraisals and other related projects of the two organizations are making a valuable contribution to the improvement of school design and construction. We believe also that the outcomes of such projects can be even more satisfactory in a functional sense for the handicapped children, teachers, and parents of the country if the guidelines in this book were given substantial weight in those decisions. There would be fewer secondary schools, for example, with a number of elevation changes on certain heavily used floors but no ramps. Grab-rails would be installed at strategic points. And there would be a sharp reduction in other architectural barriers to reasonable use of the building by handicapped persons.

American schools have not kept pace, even in the quantitative sense, with the need to supply educational space for handicapped children. The teaching space situation parallels that of teacher supply. Current national studies show an over supply of teachers *except* in special education for the handicapped, where there is a shortage in the thousands. The State of Ohio, for example, released a report in December, 1970, stating that 3,146 special education teachers were needed for 1971 to 1972 to fill new positions or positions staffed temporarily by unqualified persons. In 1974 the State of Alabama needed 500 new special education teachers, and all of the training institutions of the State, together, were graduating a total of 250.

The gap still remains, for the most part. Parallel to teacher demand, reports indicate that 19 percent of the nation's school construction in the years immediately ahead will need to focus on accommodations for exceptional children, whether incorporated in regular schools or in separate wings or buildings.

The United States Congress and the individual states are now placing high priorities on supplying school facilities for the handicapped. They have been moved by testimony demonstrating past neglect. One result is a search by architects and others for guides to plan educational space which promises to enhance the learning of handicapped pupils.

There is a problem of quality and a problem of quantity. Many existing schools are models of poor planning, rife with architectural barriers to special education. Well-intentioned but inappropriate architectural adjustments fail to improve schooling for the handicapped. And the growing trend to capitalize on new educational technology and new teaching methods to combat learning disabilities among exceptional children, and, meanwhile to keep as many of them as possible in the mainstream of education with their nonhandicapped fellow-pupils, poses new space design problems in existing elementary and secondary schools and those yet to be built.[30]

Our objective has been to produce a guide to intelligent planning. We intended to avoid technical educational matters except where germane to design and construction. When it was necessary to focus on special educational considerations, principles and illustrations are used to bridge from educational to architectural matters.

The range of the book covers the ages in which formal provisions are made for education, from infant day care centers through the college years.

We are concerned with what the teacher does and what the child does and how their operations effect the plan of a total building and its interior and exterior character.

We are concerned with space to accommodate planned learning experiences to accomplish specific educational objectives.

The points of view architects and educators have about handicaps certainly will be reflected in the construction of schools. In this book the design and construction problems are approached from the viewpoint of the learning task, how a pupil's mental, social, or body disorder requires special consideration, and how best that special consideration may be accomplished.

We acknowledge immediately and continuously the special contributions of Ralph Baird, William H. Cruickshank, Dwayne Gardner, Larry Molloy, Herbert Quay, Beatrix Sebastian and others for their conceptual contributions to the understanding of learning and the physical environment. To Henry Bertness, Samuel and Winifred Kirk, Darrel Mase, Lester Myer, Godfrey Stevens, Harvey Stevens, Maynard Reynolds, Claire B. Wilson and others, we express appreciation for their writings and conversations, so important in helping us understand exceptional children.

A serious attempt has been made to keep the technical and professional language of education used in this book consistent in meaning throughout. Three sources are used for definitions. First priority is given to *Standard Terminology for Curriculum and Instruction in Local and State School Systems.*[134] Its definitions have the endorsement of The Council for Exceptional Children, the Council of Chief State School Officers, the National School Boards Association, Inc., the United States Office of Education and ten other major educational associations and agencies. Seventy-six national agencies or organizations contributed to the work of establishing definitions. Included were fourteen groups with specific focuses on the educational and vocational rehabilitation of handicapped individuals.

If a term needing definition is not found in the above source, next priority is given to the *Dictionary of Education.*[77] Concensus statements from approximately forty special educators from the United States and Canada were responsible for establishing the meanings reported in the *Dictionary*.

In a few instances, terms were not defined in either of the above works. In those cases definitions were drawn from significant articles or books and attributed to the sources.

As noted above and elsewhere in the pages which follow, we are grateful to many who have helped us. We are particularly grateful to our students in that connection. Dr. David Kurtzman, former Chancellor of the University of Pittsburgh, once said, "I love students. They think of things that would never have come into my head." We think we know what he meant, for we have learned much from those who were supposed to be learning from us.

However, we take full responsibility for any errors of fact or interpretation others may find herein. We hope readers will tell us about them so we may, in the future, make appropriate corrections.

Jack W. Birch
B. Kenneth Johnstone

CONTENTS

CONTENTS

**DESIGNING
SCHOOLS AND SCHOOLING
FOR THE HANDICAPPED**

CHAPTER I

INTRODUCTION

U NIVERSAL EDUCATION has been promised by American law for more than a century, but only recently has it started to become a reality for handicapped children. The same legal promise of vocational rehabilitation for handicapped youth and adults has yet to be fulfilled.

Historically, handicapped children have stood last in line for desirable educational space. Their classrooms have been in outworn or obsolescent buildings, minimally modified basements, and renovated garages. In one instance, trainable retarded children in a northern region were transported to an ancient, wood-frame hut whose only heat was from open, coal-burning, pot-bellied stoves. The splintery, damp floor and the rest of the space were lit by four bare light bulbs. That *facility* was located less than 10 yards from a newly constructed elementary school costing $2.5 million dollars.*

The main reasons for the inadequacy are twofold: either no planning or poor planning has characterized educational space developed for exceptional children. Well-intentioned but inappropriate educational and architectural adjustments are failing to meet the educational needs of the exceptional children for whom the adjustments are intended. Essentially the same can be said for space and instructional procedures intended for vocational rehabilitation activities.

We view both special education and vocational rehabilitation as essentially an interaction between the person providing the service and the person receiving it. The part of the interaction which concerns us chiefly is its instructional component during which the stu-

---

*These facts can be verified in testimony given before the Committee on Education and Labor of the United States House of Representatives in the 1971 session and in the Explanatory Notes to a Bill for the Construction of Special Education Facilities submitted to the Committee in the same session.

dent or client learns useful skills or knowledge from a teacher. We believe the *where* and *how* of that interaction is of great significance. A comprehensive and thorough study has never been made of the interface of the exceptional child's educational program and his space requirements. Nor has it been done in the rehabilitation setting. Educational programs have been devised. Physical space has been designed. But few solutions have integrated program, space, and equipment into an efficient and effective whole. The first reason for inadequacy in planning, therefore, is that this emerging field is not being researched to locate, study, and specify the breakthrough landmark approaches.

The second reason that planning is inadequate is the absence, until now, of a single inclusive publication aimed at those who need the information: the teacher, the school administrator, the rehabilitation program director and the professional planner. No book existed which gave the points of view, the guidelines, the examples, and the references needed by the administrator, the teacher, the rehabilitation specialist, or by those architect-educator groups responsible for educational objectives and design of teaching space for the handicapped. Yet, they will be responsible for at least 19 percent of the school construction in the nation in the few years ahead: the 100,000 classrooms needed for the special education of exceptional children. It is our hope that this book can be a reference that will help educators and architects to fill that void of reference.

EXAMPLES OF PROBLEMS TREATED IN THE BOOK

The eight examples which follow should convey the variety and the complexity of problems considered in this book.

Example One

Emotionally disturbed children can sometimes be expected to blow their tops or climb the walls. This can happen even under expert teachers and without regard to whether the teaching method is psychodynamic or behavior shaping in style. When it happens, one of the teacher's resources (and one of the pupil's) should be a nearby, convenient, and readily supervised room in which banging, screaming, violent exercise, or other venting is harmless.

But that room cannot be a padded cell. It needs to be a setting in which the teacher is encouraged to continue instruction. Its design should help the student to maintain contact with the educational enterprise. In short, a crisis room for the education of the emotionally disturbed must be an environment responsive to the transient affective outburst; but, most of all, it must maintain its primary role as an educational environment.

Example Two

Educable mentally retarded children take longer and are older when they develop the fine, hand-eye coordinated movements needed in writing. Chalkboards in classrooms for young, educable retarded children need to extend from near the floor to 6 feet above it. This gives the teacher opportunities to apply what is known about optimum teaching of gross arm and hand movements in beginning and developmental exercises as a prelude to fine arm and hand movement.

Example Three

Handicapped children have a disproportionate share of speech defects and speech developmental lags. Speech clinicians more and more serve and help as consultants to special education teachers, and help guide speech improvement and correction activities conducted as part of the daily classroom routine. In addition, new instructional materials include large, individualized speech improvement workbooks for each child as well as other unwieldy equipment. New portable desk or tabletop, visual and auditory response machines provide pupil self-instruction under visual supervision of teachers or aides. Teaching space, shaped and packaged to support the teacher-speech clinician partnership, calls for readily accessible, independent speech practice areas minimally distracting to others and maximally convenient for teacher use and manipulation.

Example Four

Special Education is now rapidly moving into the early childhood years; so is the mainstream of education. Blind, deaf, crippled, and mentally retarded children, many with combinations of disabilities, are expected to begin schooling at two, three, and four years of age. More and more of that schooling is expected to take place in buildings where nonhandicapped preschool children are educated.

This brings enormous added problems to the teacher of the handicapped. Instruction and management of basic functions such as eating, drinking, and toileting come within the domain of the school and are shared with the home. No longer applicable are the formerly safeguarding school admission criteria of established self-care in such matters. The cognitive and affective education of the young handicapped child cannot be allowed to languish while the parents strive at home to raise the level of the youngster's personal and social functioning to the point at which feeding and toileting at school are not serious problems.

Toileting for handicapped children, for example, requires special solutions. Some will be incontinent, requiring a *clean-up* space and equipment. Doors pose problems, with a maze entry often necessary instead. For the mentally retarded, the toilet door partitions must be closer to the floor to inhibit crawling under. And in all such adaptations, two key special education and rehabilitation concepts must be in the forefront. First, the toileting situation must be designed to allow the teacher to teach the child self-help and to encourage the child to learn independent management. Second, the adaptations of setting, materials, and equipment should be the minimum necessary and should be so planned that the child will gradually be able to use closer and closer approximations of standard toileting facilities. Complete independence in the real world is the goal.

Example Five

Uneducable mentally retarded children do not learn to read and write at the level of functional literacy. But they can and should learn other very important social behaviors. An instructional area designed for the teaching of reading and writing and higher cognitive capabilities does not fit their needs. Worse, it can hold them and their teacher back. Their teaching space must encourage them to learn self-care and productive social interaction. Without proper facilities, teachers who know the objectives of education for trainable retarded children and youth are hampered in accomplishing them by conventional classrooms and sometimes even by open school space.

Example Six

The growth of personal identity or self-concept is linked with having possessions. Handicapped children need special help in acquiring wholesome ideas about themselves. Teachers who are developing the self-concepts of handicapped children need space, equipment, and instructional materials which can be allocated to such children under specific terms. Thus, the design of space calls for areas which are adaptable for individual student allotment where the student can say, "This is mine," and where actual individual possessions like books and games can be kept undisturbed.

Example Seven

The *resource room* concept was developed many years ago and was initially for the hard-of-hearing. It called for a special education classroom with a trained teacher and unique instructional materials located in a regular elementary or secondary school. There might be twenty or thirty children, hard-of-hearing in various degrees, enrolled in different grades and attending regular classes. They would repair to the *resource room* on a regular schedule and by special appointment. There they would receive initial instruction or maintenance instruction in lipreading, training in the use of amplification, special tutoring in various subjects as needed, and counseling. The special education teacher would maintain liaison with all the regular teachers, acting truly as a resource of support and assistance as needed with both professional colleagues and the pupils.

The *resource room* concept spread rapidly to special education for partially seeing pupils, blind pupils, educable mentally retarded pupils in some types of secondary schools, certain crippled and other physically handicapped children, and it has most recently caught on as a pattern for educating children with learning disabilities and children with emotional disturbances.

In all those instances, the *resource room* has certain common attributes with respect to educational programs: there is frequent coming and going, a wide range of ages must be accommodated, and complex record keeping is required. At the same time, special education objectives for *resource rooms* differ significantly. To illustrate, there are particular accessibility and mobility considerations if the *resource room* is to serve either blind children or crippled children or both. Quite different equipment and materials problems face the teacher depending also upon the specific objectives to be achieved for different groups of pupils.

Example Eight

When educable mentally retarded girls and boys reach tenth grade age at about sixteen years, the work-study part of their special education begins formally. Prior to that time, a vocational orientation appears in most curricula. But, beginning at the tenth grade level, an instructional sequence of three years can involve part-time work in school stations; half-time in community work stations and half-time in day classes; and, in the third year, full-time work in community work stations with tutoring scheduled as required. After graduation at the end of that year, when the former student is in full-time independent employment, he or she has access to the school via self-initiated appointments for special help or counseling. During this entire process, the teacher or work study coordinator is usually in contact with the counselor from the Bureau of Vocational Rehabilitation, the State Employment Office, the family of the girl or boy, and the employers and prospective employers.

The classrooms and other student areas during these years need to include real or simulated time clocks, storage lockers, and work stations. There is need for individual study or tutoring settings, availability of evening space for tutoring and counseling, space adaptable to adult meetings with parents or employers in evenings and daytime, and many other major and minor features related to the prevocational and work-study curriculum. In school, work stations are mostly real and that means that the design of the entire school is affected by the fact that there are to be student learner-helpers participating in most of the unskilled, semiskilled and skilled maintenance, kitchen and clerical work. The usual academic teaching must be facilitated by the use of space, of course, but there are added special requirements for the kinds of educational activities noted above.

It should be apparent from the above examples that this book concerns itself with the principles underlying a wide variety of complex, special educational instructional problems and issues as they relate to the space in which teachers and children meet daily. It is our hope that this book will be read and studied as a guide to thinking and conceptualizing and as an aid in problem solving.

MAIN THEMES OF THE BOOK

The three main themes of this book are presented here and will be further clarified in the chapters which follow. The themes are:

1. Common architectural barriers to total building use by the handicapped can be eliminated.
2. Subtle space adjustments can be arranged to produce significant positive impacts on quality of teaching and learning.
3. School building design should maximize the opportunity for handicapped children to stay in the mainstream of education.

It will also be shown how the effectiveness and efficiency of a specific school facility is a function of interlocks with other school facilities, and how the whole community-school complex is made up of several subsystems that are all part of a larger system.

To a very considerable extent, when the architect-educator team works on a school to accommodate handicapped pupils, it is also engaged in community planning. The community planning role is a large one, too, because schools designed to include handicapped children tend to encompass broader attendance areas. Therefore, we are concerned about the procedures which the architect and his educational colleagues may employ to increase the probability that the structure, when completed, bears an integral relationship to the total community in which it is situated. In short, the new or remodeled educational facility should be capable of optimum functioning as a subsystem of special education within the whole school system and the total, child service system of the community.

FOCUS OF THE BOOK

Teachers, school board members, school administrators, architects, and other professional specialists in planning and the lay public make up the audience for this book. All of these, and especially teachers and the lay public, need to be closely involved in the design and development of schools and schooling. Teachers are, of course, usually well represented through their professional organizations. And the lay public is also usually well represented through the school board, especially when it is an elected board. But associations and boards are generally more conservative than most of their membership, and they are motivated more by the desire to avoid mistakes than by the desire to express advanced thinking. Therefore, it is quite necessary that individual teachers and lay persons encourage their associations and boards to take more initiative than they otherwise might in moving toward more forward-looking design and development of schools and schooling.

When plans for new or remodeled buildings are being considered, a number of questions must be asked. Certainly, matters like financing, sites, and general appearance are highly important. We believe, however, that the most important questions should relate to the purposes the new or remodeled building should be expected to serve. That information should be of prime importance in determining what the new or remodeled building should be like when it is finished. The necessary constraints of cost and other related factors, then, will determine the degree to which the purposes can be realized.

So, for a school faculty these kinds of questions are paramount. What is the teacher supposed to do? What equipment is needed? How much of what is to be done by each teacher? How do these students learn best? What does the teacher require in order to do an effective job? What minimum essentials are required to achieve the teacher's purpose? What is necessary for the teacher to operate at the optimum professional level in behalf of the pupil?

This book includes significant material not found in current texts that offer introductions to special education. For our purposes, it is necessary to clarify what is expected of special education teachers and what they need to do their work well. The working conditions which allow teachers to produce excellent special education is one of our major concerns. Most current introductory books give almost all their attention to the general nature and needs of exceptional children. This is important and it is not overlooked in this book. But we have emphasized the characteristics of children which are most relevant to the work of the teacher and the setting in which that work can take place most effectively.

THE *SCHOOLHOUSE* CONCEPT

Schoolhouses must operate on two intersecting planes of reality. The first, quite simply, is that a schoolhouse is a building. It is a structure designed to provide a shelter from the elements where people can assemble to carry on the business of teaching and learning. Its skeleton, its mechanical systems, its spaces, parts and pieces must fit together in such a way as to facilitate that business. It must function efficiently, effectively, and with economy for the taxpayer.

Then there is the other reality. It has to do, rather, with the *feeling* of the schoolhouse, with the trust or lack of it that hangs in the air; with the way it conveys respect for its occupants or fails to; with the warmth or chill, the lights, shadows and textures that form the matrix in which learning takes root.

We want to create *schoolhouses* that are more responsive to the contemporary needs of the young; schoolhouses that are more sensitive, humane and more supportive of learning and growth. In essence, all of us want to equip our young with the *copeability* to live in an increasingly complex world, to enable them to contribute to the common good and to find joy in their own existence.

The behavioral sciences, and life itself, provide ample evidence that learning and growth are deeply affected by the environment in which they take place. Viewed in that light, the content of a child's education is made up of everything that happens to him from the moment he enters the *schoolhouse* to the moment he leaves.

THE FACT OF CHANGE

The whole teaching-learning continuum, which once was tied in an orderly way to the passing of generations and the growth of the child into a man—this whole process has exploded in our faces. What we have, in fact, is a 170-year-old model with a fitful history. In 1806 the English Lancastrian system of batch-process education was introduced into America. The first, fully graded public school was introduced in Boston in 1848 with the Quincy Grammar School, a school still in use. A batch of students fastened to a teacher in a box established itself as the norm for the next hundred years, and the configuration of school buildings became set in a rigid mold that is now as familiar and American as Thanksgiving turkey. Ask almost any child to draw a plan of a school, and he will draw a large box around a series of smaller, equal size boxes, set side by side.

Alterations of social patterns and life styles, and developments of new knowledge which turns even the experts into learners demand fluid educational spaces capable of responding to constant change. Who am I? Who are you? How do we relate? These are issues integral to the learning process. An environment that confuses the answers or propels people apart creates serious mischief.

Schools of the past tried to funnel a body of knowns through the teacher, the eternal talking machine. Today the best wisdom in the state of the pedagogical art asserts that quality education means reckoning with peoples' differences. It points to the diverse and individual ways children learn and teachers teach. It holds that people learn best through discovery and exploration, not by being lectured to. It views communication with other children, as well as adults, as a prime ingredient of growth. And it sees learning as a mosaic pattern made up of fragments of information from numberless sources, rather than as an unbroken linear development.

Putting these concepts into practice can mean a considerable turnaround in the way we have traditionally organized our schools. Some suggest that it means the elimination of grades and the mixing of children so the young may learn from the older and the older from teaching the young. Others say it means allowing children to work alone and together in different size groups for varying amounts of time, depending on the nature of their work. For still others it means access to a great range of media, materials, and equipment for self-instruction. And it certainly encourages teachers to join together in teams so their uneven talents can be exploited and their time more effectively engaged.

THE IMPACT OF CHANGE ON SCHOOL BUILDINGS

Clearly, such arrangements require a high degree of movement, interaction, and communication. Classroom boxes were never intended for such. They were designed for uniformity, not diversity; for a static process, not a fluid one that may shift for sound instructional reasons from hour to hour or day to day. The thrust is toward buildings that will get out of the way and permit teachers to practice the best that is known. "Schools without walls," for instance, is the first major change in the design of schoolhouses for more than a hundred years.

There seems to be a conflict of desire within us that is in a constant state of adjustment. It tries to balance on one side a powerful need to participate, to be involved with others, to be part of, to belong; against an equally powerful need to be private, individually separate, to be free from group pressures, to dominate a piece of turf ourselves. The facility that ignores or fails to recognize both sides of this tension will be unsatisfactory much of the time.

THE GENERATION RANGE

Although both adults and children occupy school facilities, there is some confusion as to what the facilities should reflect. Is it a childlike place? An adult place? Can they be combined?

Every successful living environment has a conceptual structure that precedes its physical expression. This is the statement of values and purposes that a physical facility is then designed to support. In school buildings it should be an overview that links educational and human objectives with shelter and services into one coherent effect.

THE SOCIAL CONTEXT OF SCHOOLING

Schools cannot afford to lose people. You lose people when they do not have the right places to be in.

The sensation of being in the right place is part of the constant human equation with our surroundings. In every circumstance there are individual feelings and group feelings about space. The right shape, scale, and context are always sought.

There need to be places to be:
     a single person in an egocentric context
     in two's in a companion context
     in three's or more in a social group context

in ten's to twenties in a small community context
in the hundreds in a general society context

Normal and desirable learning activity requires this spectrum of territorial places, and there is a constant effort by school populations to seek and negotiate what is needed. But it is also quite impossible in most schools for this negotiation to succeed, and a great many people feel uncomfortable and lost too much of the time. Spatial variation, negotiable by the user, is an essential language schools must provide.

THE DISPLAY FUNCTION OF THE SCHOOL

A good school is in the presentation business. It encourages the staging function of learning. It is not afraid of the tentative or naive statements of young people. It accepts them with grace.

To provide the means for handling display, the solution must deal with both aspects. First, it is necessary to assure that the environment is populated with abundant vertical surfaces frankly ready to receive graphic materials. New buildings, of course, can be designed to accept display as a basic interior esthetic, with a means for hanging and mounting built-in as an intrinsic interior detail. These can be rails, slots, button devices, and the like. Whatever the device, the point is to equip the walls in such a manner that visual materials can be buttoned into them, so to speak, or unbuttoned for quick and easy changing of exhibit items. The school client would be wise to specify this to the architect as a functional requirement.

One approach that is more satisfactory and low in cost is a concept of *graphic managers,* throwaway panels that can serve as an intermediary between the graphic object and the wall itself. These panels typically could be of treated paperboard or plastic to accept tacking, pasting, printing, painting, washing, and scraping, with a continuous lip around the perimeter for hooking onto the wall-receiving device. When they become unsightly they can be discarded.

THE SCHOOL-HOME CONTINUUM

The educational process extends into the home. Schools and homes are in a partnership that needs to be integrated and complementary. But this partnership suffers from lack of process or system.

The lack of system in the home is peculiarly destructive for the child. Throughout his school years he brings home an array of artifacts from his school work. Most often, all this is thrown away. Most homes are not organized to keep them. Often, they seem of no importance.

This material, on the contrary, is of great importance. The result of everything being thrown away has two serious effects. First, the child is taught to have a low regard for his own accomplishment, and his tangible history disappears as fast as he creates it. When he finally goes away to college, the only tangible evidence of twelve years of activity is a transcript. Parents and schools should recognize that a portion of those artifacts are of high personal value to the child and will have a place in his lifetime assessment of who he is. They must have a place to be preserved.

FREEDOM OF MOVEMENT VS. CONSTRAINTS

Opportunities for physical exuberance of the spontaneous, unscheduled kind have to be reinvented as part of educational experience. Horseplay, which is almost always suppressed, is that natural exuberance trying to find an outlet. The universal desire to dance is this impulse trying to find release. When physical activity is repressed in the classroom, it looks for an out in the demilitarized zones of the building, the hallways and cafeteria. As a consequence, behavior in these areas may become so raucous that the administrative response is to police them. This treats the symptom, not the cause, and the cycle perpetuates itself.

Both the teaching process and the school environment have to incorporate the concept of informal, natural physical movement as a frequent ingredient. What is needed are byways, wide places, and free zones within learning areas. At the absolute minimum, postural release from long periods of sitting is a must.

The idea that we manage the environment is hardly new to the homemaker who rearranges the living room or the plant manager who rearranges machines for a new product or for more efficiency. But the idea of dynamic management of the school environment is new. We have been trained to accept school interiors as setpiece statements. A school facility with the options and the permission to manipulate is a vehicle in motion. It is taking us somewhere. This is a prospect that both riders and drivers must understand, a new technology that has to do with living.

GUIDING THE CHANGES BEING MADE IN SCHOOLS

It is hard to find the person who isn't interested in improvement, in a better way of life. But who leads the decision to change?

The initiation of change is, in itself, a process in society dominated by an irreplaceable minority, the change agents. Change agents are those individuals who have a kind of venturesome self-confidence. They can and do try new things. This small group of idea testers, in turn, is watched closely by the majority. Once they adopt and endorse a new value, there is often rapid acceptance by others. Regular and special education teachers, principals and supervisors who are innovators, along with the parents and other community representatives who work with them, should be actively involved in school planning. Schools will more likely then become places where people would like to be even if they didn't have to be there.

THE MODERN SPECIAL EDUCATION TEACHER

For the first hundred years of its modern life, from 1850 to 1950, special education was dominated by orthopedic and psychiatric medicine and clinical psychology. Since about 1950, the dominant forces have been neurological and pediatric medicine and behavioristic psychology.

Teachers became free agents in determining what procedures and materials would be used in teaching during that transition. Of late, teachers have also taken on more responsibility for deciding which children need special education, the kinds of special education they need, how much shall be given, and when and where the special education should take place. In short, the teacher is emerging as the one who assesses the exceptional child's needs, decides on what special educational procedures to apply, and the one who carries out the special education plan. Where there is a team of special education teachers working with other teachers, perhaps a team including psychologists, social workers, physicians, counselors, tutors, or other aides, a special education teacher is more often being chosen to be the captain or quarterback of the team.

The modern special education teacher's position is a very responsible one. It is necessary for the teacher to know the education of children in general. Also, it is required that the teacher have competency in the specialized education of children with serious impediments to instruction.

WHAT IS EXPECTED OF THE SPECIAL EDUCATION TEACHER

What is your job with this child?

What does the school want?

What do the parents want?

The special education teacher has primary responsibility for the proper education of the pupils. It is sound, of course, for those planning new facilities to listen carefully and thoughtfully to any suggestion, from parents, from the psychologist, from the principal, or from the school custodian. All of these persons often have helpful suggestions. But the final responsibility for the exceptional child's education, what to do and how and when to do it, rests most frequently today with the special education teacher. So the teacher should be central in all planning and development of special education facilities.

It is also important not to be drawn away from the main focus, the educational objectives for the child. Often other people want the special education teacher to pay attention to their goals rather than the educational goals for children.

Any handicapped person will be better able to attain self-realization if provided with a good eductional foundation. Excellent education in technical, occupational, academic, or professional fields can compensate for other handicaps and supply the handicapped person with skills and competencies which are marketable. That is the main job of the teacher, to help the pupil attain the best and most rounded education possible. That means more than just supplying *special education* (i.e. language for the deaf, or self-control for the behaviorally disordered, or braille and mobility for the blind). It calls for *special education plus* which means special education as well as the highest quality education which any other child might receive.

ASSUMPTIONS ABOUT THE ROLE OF THE TEACHER

We have started from somewhat new assumptions, that is, that teachers are increasingly determining the nature of the work they do with pupils, that teachers have the responsibility and the competence to influence strongly the settings in which pupils are taught (buildings, rooms, facilities). Also, this book considers teachers to be the most important arbiters in educational decision making, whether in matters concerning parent-school relationships or in matters of curriculum design, methods of instruction, instructional materials, or assignments of pupils.

In order that special education teachers might live up to their responsibilities, they need more competencies and understanding than are usually found in introductory texts. This book is an initial attempt to supply that need. It has its focus on schools and schooling. This covers both current status of schools and schooling and the directions schools and schooling can be expected to take. It is our hope that the book will be particularly helpful in supplying teachers with the understanding and appreciation required to contribute to appropriate decisions about the design and development of schools and schooling for the exceptional children in the world's communities.

TEACHER AIDES

In the 1960s, the employment of teacher aides grew in acceptance. Between 1966 and 1972, the number of school districts providing aides for their teachers increased almost twofold, according to the NEA Research Bulletin.[123] In the spring of 1971, it was reported that three teachers in ten had one or more teacher aides to assist them. One in four shared an aide, while one in twenty had an aide assigned full-time.

The above figures apply to elementary and secondary teachers and schools in general. No hard data are available to specify precise ratios for special education teachers and teacher aides. It is our estimate, however, that the national ratio is about one aide for two teachers. Thus, in any planning for schooling for special education pupils, it would be advisable to design for at least a one to two aide teacher ratio.

THE WORK OF THE SPECIAL EDUCATION TEACHER

Teachers of exceptional children must be able to assess what their pupils need in order to improve educationally. That assessment process bears a relationship to what physicians have traditionally called diagnosis. The main difference is that teachers need to determine what the pupils learning situation is while the physician determines the patient's health situation.

Teachers need to plan how and in what to instruct their pupils to produce specific understanding or capabilities or to remedy learning deficits. Physicians, in a similar way, need to determine what course of treatment to apply to their patients to keep them healthy or to remedy a health deficit.

The place in which a teacher works is so important that it is often used to describe the job the teacher does. The self-contained class, the resource room, the team teaching area, and the itinerant setting are the most common. Residential schools, special day schools, and, more recently, schools where a special teacher assists regular teachers with handicapped pupils, the *mainstream,* are other locations where special education takes place.

THE SELF-CONTAINED CLASS

"I teach a self-contained class," means that the instruction is done in a room which belongs solely to one teacher and a group of pupils. All, or nearly all, of the children's instruction occurs in that room. Sometimes a teacher setting is so self-contained that it has its own wash room, bathroom, conference room, lockers and supply area, and is, to all intents, a suite.

Self-contained classes have been used in teaching all sorts of exceptional children. As special education became a more and more accepted part of public education during the period from 1900 to 1930, almost all classes in the public schools were self-contained. At that time it was customary to find special classes in regular public schools for children with *lowered vitality* who were thought to be particularly susceptible to tuberculosis and other debilitating diseases; special classes for children with academic deficiencies, often called *restoration* or *remedial* classes; classes for crippled children; and special classes for children who were mentally retarded in the educable range. The latter classes were often called *opportunity classes,* or classes for the orthogenically retarded, or *Binet* classes, as well as classes for the educable mentally retarded.

The desirability of the self-contained class has been questioned more and more in the past forty years. It has been thought more educationally advisable and more economically practicable to move toward open instructional settings. With few exceptions (and they will be pointed out later) the self-contained classroom or suite in public schools is now considered a less satisfactory instructional arrangement than other settings like resource rooms and team teaching areas.

This is not to say that the self-contained classroom cannot be used effectively in teaching. Far from it: the self-contained room or suite can house a very good instructional program for almost any group of exceptional or other children. But it is no longer a necessary arrangement; and it is more difficult to attain excellence at a reasonable cost there than it is, for example, when a combination of regular classroom and resource room or some other arrangements are used.

THE *RESOURCE ROOM* CONCEPT

More than a quarter of a century ago advances in knowledge about how to organize classrooms and schools for instruction began to bring children with learning disabilities and behavior disorders into public schools and out of confinement to their homes, psychiatric hospitals, special residential schools, or child guidance clinics. The resource room, a central room in the regular school designed to accommodate youngsters when they needed special tutoring or reassurance, began to be used to minimize disruptive behavior outbursts and academic failure in regular classrooms. The availability of resource rooms and teachers as needed now allows many exceptional children to be educated in regular schools.

The resource room was first used on a large scale for hard-of-hearing children and partially-seeing children. Such centers could be found frequently in large city elementary and secondary schools by 1935. The special help of the resource teachers was employed for individualized supportive instruction, using the special resources housed in the resource room (large type books and typewriters for the visually handicapped and language and speech tutoring and instruction in hearing). By approximately 1940, the resource room came into use for crippled children (John Marshall High School, Minneapolis, and the Casis Elementary School, Austin, Texas). Still later by 1950, the resource room concept began to be used for children with learning disabilities and/or behavior disorders.

ITINERANT TEACHERS

Itinerant teachers, for music and art particularly, were frequently used as early as 1900 both within and among regular schools. But the time of the change, from bringing handicapped children to a central school to taking the special education services to the child in his own school by way of an itinerant teacher, is not documented. It is not clear, for example, when the speech correctionist first left the clinic and began to go from school to school to give speech correction instruction. It was a well-established practice, however, in 1930 in larger cities in the United States. The invention (or adoption) of an itinerant teacher service model for speech handicapped children was paralleled by similar, special education travelling teachers, services to visually handicapped children in regular school classrooms. More recently, attempts are being made, especially in sparsely populated areas (i.e. Vermont), to supply more kinds of special education in that fashion using teachers prepared in more than one aspect of special education.

THE SCHOOL IN THE HOSPITAL

Any hospital which admits children for more than a few days is now considered incomplete if it has no facilities for carrying on the youngster's schooling. Absence from school can have devastating effects. The negative effect of absence can be multiplied by hospitalization.

There are three effective special education adjustments for hospitals which admit children on a short-term basis up to three months. For longer stretches, school arrangements are discussed under the heading of "residential schools."

The three hospital-school arrangements are:

1. Personal Bedside Teaching.
2. Telephone Bedside Teaching.
3. Schoolroom in the Hospital.

Personal bedside teaching service usually comes from the local school system. If the hospital is in the school district of the child's residence, administration is simpler, but it can work even if the hospital is distant.

Someone at the hospital is usually assigned the responsibility of discovering the child's school and principal and of making an immediate contact to ascertain what schooling arrangement is to be made. Modern hospitals, often as part of the admission routine, give parents information booklets which, among other things, indicate how continuation of schooling is assured.

RESIDENTIAL SCHOOLS

Typically, the early residential schools were for crippled children, blind children, deaf children, mentally retarded children, or behavior problem children, the latter being then more often called delinquent children. Each group had their own schools.

Residential schools and day schools are still being developed, though at a much diminished rate and for substantially different special educational purposes. The change is occasioned largely because of two developments: (1) more sophisticated teaching methods and materials now allow many handicapped children to receive excellent educational opportunities in regular schools; and (2) special residential schools now cater to severely handicapped, retarded children (i.e. Central Colony, Madison, Wisconsin) or to children who have multiple handicaps such as blindness coupled with crippling conditions, hearing losses, mental retardation, or emotional disturbances.

Many residential schools were originally designed for the comprehensive education of one relatively uncomplicated group like blind children or deaf children of average or above intelligence without other handicaps. Such schools are now changing radically. They no longer receive as many uncomplicated pupils, for such youngsters are being educated in their home communities. Instead, residential school enrollments now contain large numbers of multiply handicapped pupils.

SPECIAL DAY SCHOOLS

Separate day schools for crippled children and others were also constructed, particularly during the 1920s and 1930s and usually in larger cities and heavily populated metropolitan areas. Transportation from home to school and meals at school were furnished wholly or partly at public expense. In the case of crippled children this move was accomplished by the development of specially designed vehicles.

MAINSTREAMING (INCLUSION IN REGULAR CLASSES)

PUPIL: He goes to the *special class.*
TEACHER: I teach *special class.*
PARENT: I don't want my child in any *special class!*

Recently in a small community school, a principal told us that an official from the State Education Agency had all but ruined the excellent work going on in an elementary school with educable mentally retarded pupils simply by referring to the children by that title. While saying complementary things to a newspaper reporter, the State official spoke of the "educable mentally retarded" children being helped, and he was quoted in a news story. By telephone and in person, parents demanded the removal of their children. Curiously enough, they all did so regretfully, for they liked what had been happening with their children. But they didn't want their youngsters, who were "slow and in need of special help," to be unduly influenced by associating with "mentally retarded" children. The principal and teachers of that school had, up to that time, used only educationally relevant language in speaking of "special instruction," giving "individualized teaching," recognizing the need to "teach carefully and thoroughly, even tho' at a slower pace," and the like, without apparently needing to use labels.

There have been *special classes* doing effective work in American schools for more than fifty years. Actually, as noted earlier, they were intended to accommodate children with chronic health problems, children with hearing or vision handicaps, and many others, each in his own group. But the term *special class* has, in many communities, come to be associated mainly with programs for educable retarded pupils. And it is now all too often considered an opprobrious term. This is one of the reasons why some communities are attempting to provide special education without special classes.

In many cases, it is now feasible to bring special education to handicapped pupils without removing the pupils from the regular grades to which they are assigned. Special education is more portable than it was. Individually constructed teacher-made instructional materials are giving way to excellent mass-produced products. Teaching methods are more refined, more standardized, and less dependent on individual artistry. Thus, many special education teachers carry out most of their work in the context of regular classes as a member of a team of teachers.

TOWARD A MORE FLEXIBLE VIEW OF APTITUDE

Special education teachers are taking a more flexible, a more dynamic view of aptitude. The *aptitude* concept, improperly applied, can be counter productive. Aptitude based schools are those which consider learning capacity or intelligence as unchangeable, so they can easily become simply sorting and selecting agencies. In such a school teachers come to say, "Last year's class was a good one," or, "That section is the dummies." Unfortunately, for many years special education contributed to the improper application of the *aptitude* concept. Special education was long dominated by the formula:

1. Find a measure of the pupil's aptitude (intelligence).
2. Teach in terms of the measured aptitude (intelligence).

Now special education is responding to a different formula:

1. a. Find the pupil's low spots in achievement (deficits).
   b. Teach intensively to correct them (remedy).
2. a. Find the pupil's high spots in achievement (assets).
   b. Teach extensively to enhance them (extend).
3. Do both (1) and (2) concurrently.

The newer special education formulation is more dynamic. It is more complex. It calls for more decision making by the teacher and a wider range of instructional methods and materials options. It is more demanding to manage. And it calls for space and facilities of a different sort than did the older, more static formulation of instruction.

THE TEACHER'S CHIEF FUNCTION

Put in operational terms, the teacher's function is to set educational objectives, to determine how near the pupil is to attaining those objectives, to teach so as to close the gap, and then repeat the process. The situation can be diagrammed symbolically in arithmetical form like a subtraction problem as follows:

$$\begin{array}{l} \text{Educational Objective (Expected Final Result)} \\ - \text{ Pupil's Present Status (Entry Level)} \\ \hline \text{Performance Gap (What Needs to be Taught)} \end{array}$$

The result of the above subtraction is the problem which faces the teacher.

The above is very much a simplification, of course. But it is essentially accurate, and it does provide a jumping-off place for the work leading to preparing educational specifications for a school program. It must be borne in mind that teachers have literally hundreds of bits of *performance gap* data to be dealt with daily, and they must be fitted into a continuum of instruction. And it must be remembered that the teacher's job will not be accomplished without instructional materials that are suited to the task, high in interest, and manageable by teacher and student; and a suitable place in which to carry on the instruction; and skill on the teacher's part in putting those elements together for effective instruction. That is our operational definition of a setting for good teaching.

CORRECTION OF DEVELOPMENTAL LAGS

A major emphasis in contemporary special education is the correction of developmental lags. That is true regardless of the age of the child, but it is especially true of work with young children where intervention of that kind is considered most effective. Modern educational assessment tools for very young children (Denver Developmental Schedule; Vineland Social Maturity Scale) allow teachers to discover slowdowns in intellectual, motor, and social development which could later presage learning disabilities. When evidence of such developmental delays is found, educational programs are mounted to correct or ameliorate them.

Special educators are able to point out the most common kinds of instructional settings called for in the correction of developmental lags. Sometimes there is need for quiet, such as separated space for a child to work alone on individualized materials or equipment. Sometimes space is required for peer teaching, where one child helps instruct another.

REHABILITATION

In the broadest sense, everything that is done to help normalize life for a handicapped individual can be considered rehabilitation or habilitation. We appreciate and accept that viewpoint. Practically speaking, however, we are limiting this book to a focus on special education. We give no direct consideration to social rehabilitation, vocational rehabilitation, or medical rehabilitation as such.

At the same time, almost everything that is said about special education has meaning for other aspects of habilitation or rehabilitation. In principle, the same considerations regarding mobility, socialization, and other aspects of personal and group living apply in all settings. So whether one is preoccupied with the victims of traumatic physical injuries, the aging processes, antisocial or criminal behaviors, mental illnesses, chronic illnesses, socio-economic or culture born deprivations, or any other limiting conditions, the concepts illustrated in this book can be adapted and applied. In each case, there is an interface between the space or setting and the human activities involved in the rehabilitation process. And thoughtful attention on the part of architects and practicing professionals in any aspect of rehabilitation can increase the probability that the client will be better served.

CHAPTER II

SPECIAL EDUCATION'S RELATION TO EDUCATION AS A WHOLE

FORMAL EDUCATION in America and in most parts of the world is a vast undertaking which involves all children and youth in certain age groups. Special education takes place in the context of the formal education of all children. It is the interaction and interrelationships of the two, with special reference to the designing of schools and schooling, which makes up the content of this chapter.

Education, as we view it, is much more general than schooling. Realistically, education takes place at the mother's knee long before children start attending schools. And education goes on in that same general sense outside of schools and after school attendance ceases.

It is the *in-school* experience, what we call *formal education*, which makes up the content of this book, along with the articulation between in-school and out-of-school learning during the period of formal school attendance. Schooling, and the setting in which it takes place, should blend smoothly into the rest of life. At the same time it should have a character of its own.

THE PURPOSE OF EDUCATION IN THE UNITED STATES

There are unique statements to be made concerning the education of handicapped children and youth. But they must be made in the context of a broader social philosophy which considers schooling important for everyone.

Schools and schooling today have more dynamic roles in society than they had in the days when the chief functions of education were (a) to pass on cultural and national heritages and (b) to produce a literate electorate. Education now has added responsibilities.

1. American education is expected to provide schooling for children

and youth which strengthens their understanding, appreciation, and capability for achievement in a democratic society.

2. Education aims at moving society away from reliance on the predominant and prevailing culture toward a broader and pluralistic cultural base.

3. Schools are expected to teach pupils to challenge questionable practices and to remedy the culture born learning deficiencies of disadvantaged children and youth, thereby improving the quality of life in all segments of the nation.

4. Public education, particularly, is intended to prepare students to be usefully employed upon completion of secondary school or to obtain further systematic education, with the result that all students have marketable occupational competencies whenever they separate from the formal educational system.

5. The educational program for each student is to be designed to foster and increase self-development and self-fulfillment, with the major weight being upon the preeminence of the individual, while safeguarding the rights of all to the guarantees of equal protection under law.

The above responsibilities of education do involve transmission of the common cultural heritage from the past. In the broad sense, the cultural heritage includes the ever present potentiality of citizens to change the cultural structure, should the majority so desire. There can be no question, however, that contemporary education agencies are also being called upon to express the will of today's generation more than ever before.

OBJECTIVES OF EDUCATION IN THE UNITED STATES

The fact that education in this country is an individual state matter rather than a national responsibility has made it difficult to obtain concensus on the objectives of education. Despite that, over the past seventy-five years at least four sets of statements pertaining to objectives have gained widespread acceptance among professional educators. The earliest was in 1918 and the most recent was in 1966. They are listed in the following table. An attempt has been made to position the statements so those with similar appearing concepts can be read across horizontally. It will be noted that some themes

Table I

FOUR STATEMENTS OF EDUCATIONAL OBJECTIVES IN THE UNITED STATES

1918 Seven Cardinal Principles*	1938 Four Groups of Objectives †	1952 Ten Imperative Needs ‡	1966 Imperatives in Education §
1. Worthy home membership		1. Family life	1. To discover and nuture creative talent
2. Health		2. Health	2. To make urban life satisfying
3. Command of fundamental processes	1. Self-realization	3. Ability to think and communicate clearly	3. To strengthen the moral fabric of society
		4. Arts (esthetics)	4. To deal constructively with psychological tensions
		5. Science	5. To make intelligent use of resources
4. Worthy use of leisure time		6. Use of leisure	6. To make the best use of leisure time
5. Vocation	2. Economic efficiency	7. Occupational skill	7. To prepare people for the world of work
		8. Ability to consume wisely	8. To keep democracy working
6. Citizenship	3. Civic responsibility	9. Civic understanding	9. To work with other peoples of the world for human betterment
7. Ethical character	4. Human relations	10. Human relations	

* National Education Association, *Cardinal Principles of Secondary Education*, bulletin 35, U.S. Bureau of Education, GPO, Commission Reorganization of Secondary Education, 1918.

† Educational Policies Commission, National Education Association, *The Purposes of Education in an American Democracy*, Washington, The Association, 1938.

‡ Educational Policies Commission, National Education Association, *Education for All American Youth: A Further Look*, Washington, The Association, 1954.

§ American Association of School Administrators, *Imperatives in Education*, Report of the AASA Commission on Imperatives in Education, Washington, The Association, 1966.

involving the home, health, personal development, citizenship, human relations, and self-support achievement seem to recur, regardless of how people expressed them at different periods in our recent history.

These general statements about what education should help pupils accomplish apply to all students, handicapped or not. It is plain, of course, that the objectives people set cannot always be fully attained. This is most obvious in the case of handicapped persons. But it remains true that equality of educational opportunity requires that *all* pupils have the right to attempt to reach those objectives; moreover, they have the right to specialized instruction, should that be necessary, to assure that they have every chance to overcome or by-pass their handicaps.

In later sections, as certain groups of handicaps are described, the discussion will include particularized educational objectives for special education.

EXPANDING EDUCATION FACILITIES FOR HANDICAPPED PUPILS

In 1974, litigation was under way in at least twenty states in the United States where parents were bringing suit for denial to their handicapped children of "equal protection" under the Fourteenth Amendment. Many of their handicapped children, they claimed, were excluded from school on the grounds that there was no provision for them.

A representative of The Council for Exceptional Children, A. R. Abeson, held that 60 percent of the seven million handicapped children in the United States were receiving no public education in 1973. The remainder received some degree of service.

Handicapped children have been held by the legislature and courts of the states and the federal structure* to be entitled to be equal participants in and equal beneficiaries of the above educational goals. We observe an increasing effort, nationally, to make that happen. It is yet far from a fully effective effort, but it is growing.

---

*In the U.S. District Court for the Eastern District of Pennsylvania. *Pennsylvania Association for Retarded Children, Nancy Beth Bowman, et al. Plaintiff vs., Commonwealth of Pennsylvania, David H. Kurtzman, et al. Defendants.* Civil Action No. 71-42 Amended Consent Agreement, 14 February 1972.

Court rulings now affirm that a lack of financial resources is no acceptable excuse for failure of a school district to provide special education. One effect of those rulings is accelerated growth now and in the immediate future of facilities for exceptional pupils.

SPECIAL EDUCATION AROUND THE WORLD

In European countries, both eastern and western, special education is found as a partner with standard education. The same is true in New Zealand, Australia, the Philippines, and the Trust Territories of the Pacific. The Far East has been a little slower to develop special education, but it is growing. The same can be said for the Middle East and most of Africa, where the development is somewhat slow and uneven. Canada has a very well defined special education effort, and Mexico has made substantial progress in that direction. The Central and South American nations have also shown strong interest in program development too in recent years. Worldwide, the countries which have moved toward compulsory, universal education for their young citizens recognize that programs of special education are a necessity if all persons are to have equal educational opportunity.

SPECIAL EDUCATION AT THE NATIONAL LEVEL IN THE U.S.A.

On constitutional grounds the federal role in public and private education is very limited because education is primarily a state function. The United States constitution itself does not mention education. The Tenth Amendment, part of the "Bill of Rights" added to the Constitution in 1791, placed education under the responsibility and authority of the several states.

There has been steadily increasing interest in education on the part of the Federal Congress and on the part of the Executive Branch in the years since the Second World War. The evidence of increased Congressional interest began with a one million dollar Cooperative Research Act. Its passage was spearheaded by the National Association for Retarded Children, the Council for Exceptional Children, and several other national volunteer and professional organizations.

Since then, congressional and administrative interest has fostered significant leadership at the federal level, including the federal regional offices. The organizational chart of the Department of Health, Education and Welfare's U.S. Office of Education is not reproduced here, for it varies with shifting emphasis in the federal administration, and it is truly a vast and complex governmental unit.

Inside the U.S. Office of Education is the Bureau of Education for the Handicapped. Its organizational chart also is altered from time to time. However, its functions do not change markedly.

The chief functions of the Bureau of Education of the Handicapped are:

1. Research on the improvement of special education.
2. Training of teachers and other educational specialists for special education activities.
3. Services to strengthen state departments of education in special education.
4. Information gathering and dissemination on special education.
5. Consultation to public and private special education agencies.

The federal governmental effort in special education, concentrated mainly in the Bureau for the Education of the Handicapped, is important, and it is growing.

Taken together, the 1972 fiscal year expenditures by the Federal Government for all of education amounted to approximately four billion dollars. For the same fiscal year, states spent from their own funds approximately twenty-one billion dollars, and local school systems spent from local tax funds about twenty-seven billion dollars. As of 1972, the Federal Government's contribution to public education was about 7.8 percent of the total cost.

STATE EDUCATION AGENCIES

State education agencies in the United States of America decide what form special education will take in their respective states. There are very great differences from state to state. The differences extend to such fundamental matters as the following, among others:

1. Local or regional units responsible for special education.
2. Which children are recognized as needing special education.

3. What kinds of teachers are needed, and the nature of the preparation teachers should have.
4. The minimum and maximum ages of pupils entitled to free public education.
5. The extent of financial support for educating handicapped pupils.
6. What kinds of school building and equipment and facilities can be authorized.
7. The nature of the curriculum and instructional materials which may be used.
8. The degree to which special education is mandatory.

Differences among states in these matters are great. The laws and regulations also change frequently because states are constantly trying to improve their special education. Therefore, no specific examples of state plans are included here. They could be out of date before a book could be printed and distributed.

But it is imperative to be knowledgeable about the special education regulations of the state in which your activities with exceptional children are to be carried on. That holds for parents, teachers, teachers-in-training, school board members, and others whose work or personal life has a special education component. It is particularly important to children who themselves require special education services. They and their families should be informed by their teachers and others about the nature of their state's special education regulations and about their rights under those provisions. Certainly, also, no teacher or principal or other member of the support staff or administration can be fully effective without detailed knowledge of what the state education agency has determined shall constitute special education within the bounds of its jurisdiction. The regulations are free and may be obtained by writing to the proper office.

What has been said about states in the United States can be applied in general to the provinces of Canada. In most other countries, however, the responsibility and authority for special education tends to be concentrated at the national level.

CHAPTER III

HOW HANDICAPPED CHILDREN ARE EDUCATED

TOO OFTEN AT THE START of the development of a new facility for special education, the responsible educational staff and the architect take off as though there had never before been any special education facilities designed. A much more desirable approach is to plan forward from what is already established. In very few instances will the design team be working in a *de nova* situation. They need to be sure they are familiar with what already exists. There is no need to *discover America* anew with each building or remodeling project for accommodating education to handicapped pupils.

Modern special education for children with serious educational problems has a rich history. Today's handicapped children benefit from educational inventors long past.

Mentally retarded pupils are now taught by refinements of methods suggested by Itard and Binet.[98] Those early workers developed what can now be recognized as primitive individualized instruction schemes based on selecting specific behavioral objectives. They then attempted to teach toward the objectives they had selected.

Deaf and hard-of-hearing children today learn by procedures which rely on the early work of Bell [98] who pioneered amplification which allowed persons with impaired hearing to receive sounds they would otherwise miss. Other pioneers organized and codified manual signs which produced a visual language system for those who could not hear.[98]

Blind children receive special education based on a tactual communication system invented by Braille.[98] More recent improvements in enlargement of type and advances in the use of magnifying lenses to maximize what residual eyesight is present gives added reading capability to children who would otherwise have needed to rely upon braille alone.

There are full reports on the history of special education. The purpose here is simply to bring into focus the following points:

1. There is a substantial history of special education dating back more than one hundred years.
2. Early developments in special education are in use today, many with only relatively minor modification from the original.
3. Modern procedures and approaches for certain handicapped children, resource rooms for children with learning disabilities, for example, are sometimes made possible by new uses of well-established procedures already in use for children with other kinds of educational handicaps.
4. There is a considerable background of cross-fertilization between education for exceptional children and education for all other children.
5. Special education is continuing to change, with new moves being stimulated by new educational inventions and technological developments.

Architects cannot be expected to know "what is old, and what is new; what is tried and what is true" about special education. Neither, for that matter, can most educators whose careers have been spent isolated from work with handicapped pupils.

Architects and regular educators are eager to learn what is useful about special education's body of knowledge, however. They do not want to make mistakes, and they do not want to waste time and resources exploring ground which has already been mapped by someone else. So, it is the responsibility of the special educators on the planning team to make sure that available knowledge is applied in direct or adapted form.

Recent History

Today a great deal more is known about the effects of people and surroundings on each other. A more human spirit has grown, following, if not in parallel with, the technological advances which have been most noticeable in the twentieth century. The flowering of the behavioral sciences during the same period supplied research techniques which, motivated by desires for a better life for everyone, were applied to such questions as how to assure a happy fit between people and things, both at work and elsewhere.

The results are only beginning to be applied to education. And the application follows a precedent established in recent years, namely, improvements in instructional technology and processes frequently have their origins in special education for the handicapped and are subsequently adapted and adopted for all children. Below is a partial list of such technological and process advances which had their beginnings in programs for the handicapped and now represent prevailing practices for all schools. Some advances are:

1. Clinical teaching (one-to-one, tutorial instruction).
2. Diagnosis of pupil's specific learning needs.
3. Adequate standard of intensity of light with minimum glare on work surfaces.
4. Unit of instruction approach based on children's needs.
5. Grouping for instruction.
6. Use of psychological consultant services for teacher.
7. Use of school social work services for school-home-community liaison.
8. Development of instructional materials designed to meet special needs.

The ultimate goal of programs for handicapped persons is not stereotyping but normalization. Each human lives an unique life, and each life is lived within some societal boundaries. There is a broad area within socially acceptable bounds that is *normal*. The process called normalization is one which, hopefully, makes it feasible for a handicapped person to learn to participate effectively within those bounds, to be a normal individual.

There is no contradiction of terms here. Each handicapped person must achieve self-realization. That is not necessarily done by aping nonhandicapped persons. It is accomplished by becoming self-sufficient, self-reliant, self-respecting; literally by building a *self* which can coexist with all others with independence equivalent to that shown by others. When that is achieved, normalization has been attained.

CHILDREN NEEDING SPECIAL EDUCATIONAL RESOURCES

Several principles guide consideration of the number and the nature of exceptional children in any school population. Whoever is in charge of special education should make specific numerical data available as part of the educational program data from which an architect will work.

However, the data must be tempered by the realization that a school has a long life and student population conditions can change during the building's lifetime. So, those in charge of special education need to supply not only current demographic information but also five, ten, twenty, and thirty year projections. This has an inevitable degree of risk, to be sure. However, anyone who cares to compare 1940 and 1970 will find that there was *no diminution* in the need for special education during that period of time. Thus, it would be inappropriate on the basis of past experience to expect the problem to go away in the foreseeable future. Therefore, the first principle for making projections is:

1. Expect at least the same need for special education in the future if the total demographic picture of the population served by the school does not change substantially.

The proviso concerning possible population change in the first principle leads to the second principle, namely:

2. The lower the socio-economic level of the school community in relation to surrounding communities, the larger will be the proportion of handicapped pupils.

The converse of that is also true. However, the highest socio-economic neighborhoods have a share of exceptional children, too. The nature of exceptional children, though, tends to shift with the level of wealth in the community. That leads to a third principle:

3. Retarded, crippled, and sensory handicapped conditions increase as the socio-economic level goes down, and emotional disturbances and giftedness among children increase as the socio-economic level goes up.

The above three principles are recommended for consideration when making needed projections. They are empirically determined principles, grounded in data from experience. It is important to point out that they are not reflections of the social philosophy of those who use them. Rather, it is an acknowledgment that, in this imperfect world, there are negative environmental conditions which have limiting effects on children and that there are positive environmental situations which enhance the development of children.

The procedures which are used to make projections of special education needs should be stated in the educational program document. For example, one could make linear projections on the basis of published percentages of incidence of conditions which usually call for special education. As of 1970, the Bureau of Education for the Handicapped, U.S. Office of Education, used the following percentages:

Speech Impaired	3.5	percent
Emotionally Disturbed	2.0	percent
Mentally Retarded	2.3	percent
Learning Disabled	1.0	percent
Hard-of-Hearing	0.5	percent
Deaf	0.075	percent
Crippled or other Health Impaired	0.5	percent
Visually Impaired	0.1	percent
Multihandicapped	0.06	percent
Total	10.035	percent

Those percentages are national. There can be significant fluctuations from one locality to another. A procedure for making projections based on local data is described in a report by J. W. Birch in the March, 1970, issue of the Newsletter of the Council of Administrators of Special Education.[29]

In a number of instances state education agencies have adopted percentage figures to be used in estimating special education's needs. These are particularly useful because they are couched in the special education terminology of the given states for even in neighboring states, Ohio and Pennsylvania and West Virginia, for example, there are important differences in the terms and definitions used to refer to pupils who are considered *eligible* for special education. Such terms and definitions primarily serve an accounting function in that they allow counts to be made which, in turn, have a relation to state and local budgeting and financing for special education. It is, therefore, quite important that need projections be made in language compatible with state terminology. Serious differences in technical terminology could jeopardize state approval of construction plans and could influence the state's participation in financing the projected instructional program.

SPECIAL EDUCATION: A NON-SYSTEM

As indicated earlier, special education for exceptional children can be found in all parts of America and in most parts of the world. It would be inaccurate to speak of it as a system of education, however. A system is characterized by orderliness, comprehensiveness, and a unitary quality; it is an ordered and inclusive assemblage of parts, however complex, forming regular and predictable arrangements. Special education is, at present, a conglomerate rather than a system. There is little evidence of order in either its sponsorship, its procedures, or its structure.

Special education does have a common purpose. Wherever it is found, special education attempts to either (a) correct educational deficiencies to the extent that people can make satisfactory progress on their own in the main stream of education or (b) produce and maintain maximum correction of educational deficiencies, even though that may be short of restoring pupils to independent participation in regular classrooms. In the latter case, ideally, special educational help for pupils is continued throughout their school career, always keeping the pupils as much as possible a part of the program for their nonhandicapped peers. Also, ideally, advantage is taken of every new teaching procedure and every improvement in teaching facilities, equipment, and materials in order to move exceptional children nearer to complete correction in the educational sense.

HOW SPECIAL EDUCATION IS PROVIDED

If one were a parent faced with the problem of finding educational facilities for a handicapped child in a community in the United States or elsewhere, the approach would need to be somewhat different from that taken for a child without a handicap. For non-handicapped pupils, parents could rely upon the fact that every community contains a system of free public schools extending from first grade through twelfth grade, often including kindergarten at the beginning and a variety of types of secondary schooling and even public community colleges at the other end. Such a systematic arrangement is far from commonplace with the nonsystem of special education in the United States and some other countries.

A practical first step a parent might take in looking for special education would be to inquire at the main office of the local school system and ask for the individual responsible for education for handicapped pupils. That might be a person with one of the following titles:

1. Director of Special Education.
2. Director of Pupil Personnel Services.
3. Supervisor of Special Education.
4. Coordinator of Special Education.
5. School Psychologist.

Once that individual is located and the problem explained, the most probable next step would be the arrangement for some form of assessment for the child by the person in charge and the parent.

The assessment usually consists of examinations by educational diagnosticians, psychologists, specialized physicians, and others, usually in the full-time employ of the schools or serving as part-time consultants. The assessment is free of charge and is a prelude to enrollment of the child in the most appropriate special education program, the one most likely to correct or ameliorate the educational problem presented by the child. In this connection it is preferred practice for school personnel to discuss the results of the assessment with the adults who are responsible for the child and to obtain their concurrence and support in the special education plan to be instituted. Only after agreement is reached between school personnel and the family would the child's special education be started.

There is less uniformity in educational practice from school district to school district for handicapped children than for other children in all respects. Transfer of a third grader or ninth grader from a school in one community to a school in another is not always without its problems, but it is simplicity itself compared to the same move for a handicapped child.

In some communities (e.g. Plano, Texas; Tacoma, Washington; Tucson, Arizona) the pupil would probably attend a regular school near his home, usually the one attended by brothers and sisters. In such communities, the special education programs are largely integrated into the schools attended by nonhandicapped students.

In other locations (e.g. Reading, Pennsylvania; St. Louis County, Missouri) the special education pupils are very often congregated in special day school centers. These schools serve large areas, and the children are transported by bus.

In still other communities, certain handicapping conditions are more commonly found in separate schools, and others are integrated into regular schools. There is no firm rule as to which is which, but the more common divisions are as follows:

SELDOM SEGREGATED	OFTEN SEGREGATED
Speech Handicapped	Deaf
Educable Mentally Retarded	Crippled
Hard-of-hearing	Blind
Partially Seeing	Trainable Mentally Retarded
Learning Disability/Behavior Disorder	

Another factor which appears to play an important role in determining whether special education is physically integrated with other education is population density. In less dense areas, individual schools tend to be smaller and not so near the homes of pupils. Since handicapped children are small minority groups, it has traditionally been considered necessary to transport them from various parts of a region in order to accumulate enough at some central point to make it feasible to mount all the facilities and staff necessary for a good special education program for them. A substantial change from that style of organization has been growing in popularity. Called inclusion or mainstreaming, it is an approach which takes special education to the handicapped child, wherever he is. That is discussed in other sections of this book.

An additional factor which complicates the question about which exceptional children are educated where, is the presence or absence of other highly specialized schools. In Pittsburgh, for example, there has long been a residential school for blind children in the heart of the city. Years ago, that school began an outreach program which transported blind children from the city and environs each day by taxi. The educational program was satisfying to parents, community, and school authorities. Thus, there was little reason to have special education programs for blind children mounted by the city or suburban schools on their own. But in Atlanta the opposite was the case. The special school was a considerable distance from the city. In consequence, there was parental and professional pressure to initiate special education for the blind pupils of Atlanta within the city schools. As a result, Atlanta is known as an exemplary location for the integration of blind pupils into regular schools, with special education services brought to them there.

Such factors as those briefly noted above contribute to state, regional and local differences in the ways special education reaches consumers. It is important that those kinds of factors be known to the educators, architects, and others involved in planning, and that their influences be taken into account.

In the United States, special education opportunities are supplied by local public schools, private nonsectarian schools, parochial schools, private volunteer associations, state agencies, and the federal government. There are parallels to that, of course, in education for all children and youth. But sometimes the nonpublic schools are the only ones available to handicapped children, whereas nonhandicapped children almost always have a choice. The lack of options for the handicapped child results from the failure, so far, of state governments to live up fully to their responsibilities and commitments regarding equal educational opportunity for all children.

There is, therefore, often a sizable gap between what handicapped children are entitled to educationally and what they actually receive. That gap is closing, but it has a long way to go.

There is less uniformity from school district to school district for handicapped children than for others. Within a state, the school districts are supposed to provide very similar services and follow very similar procedures. It is not uncommon, however, to find that two otherwise comparable communities may be at extremes with respect to supplying very rich or very meagre fare for handicapped children.

It can be even worse when comparisons are made across state lines. Since education in America is a state function, and since various approaches to special education have their advocates, it is not unusual to have the same child called educable mentally retarded in the regulations of one state, brain injured in another state, emotionally disturbed in another state, learning disabled in another, and neurologically handicapped in still another. Moreover, the organization and conduct of the special education programs can vary as much as the terms used to designate the handicapping conditions suggest.

Strong efforts have been made to bring about more order. These have ranged from the development of common terminology [134] to attempts for agreement upon a taxonomy of educational objectives.[149] To date, such efforts have succeeded mainly in creating more awareness of the differences that exist; unanimity on objectives, procedures, evaluation, or language is still more a hope than a reality.

Special education is certainly a part of the whole of education in each state of the United States and in many countries. Yet, special education cannot be viewed as a system. It is better understood as a group of very different educational services with common purposes but great variability in delivery capability. Key points which emerge from a review of its present nonsystematic condition are:

1. All special education has common purposes which focus on the correction or amelioration of educational deficiencies.
2. Special education is hard put to keep its prevailing practices consistent with new knowledge about preferred practices.
3. There are substantial differences in the amount and quality of special education from one part of a state to another and from state to state.
4. Enrollment of a child in a special education program calls for a different set of procedures from enrollment in other school programs.
5. Delivery procedures for special education differ from place to place in ways which are not readily predictable.
6. Efforts are being made to move special education toward being a system.

CHAPTER IV

THE INFLUENCE OF SPACE ON LEARNING

PERHAPS THE EARLIEST historical evidence that human behavior and space do interact in predictable ways was the removal of criminals and insane persons from the free and open environment of the society in general. That was almost certainly a move to protect others from the depredations of criminals and from the unpredictable acts of the mentally ill.

The places where law violators and the mentally unstable were first lodged also illustrate an historical lesson. It seems clear that small cells, lack of sunlight, sparse furniture, no heat, and primitive amenities spelled punishment. Those earliest instances demonstrate that our ancestors had learned that a harsh, restricted, and uncomfortable environment would be punishing to its inhabitants. So, protection from danger for the larger society and punishment for the wrongdoers was achieved at one and the same time by straightforward alteration of environment and facilities.

Perhaps without being explicitly aware of the above concept, educators in recent decades have produced such changes as those listed below to improve schools and schooling:

1. Movable furniture in classrooms.
2. Physical education adapted to individual student needs.
3. Occupational-vocational-technical education begun in the elementary grades.
4. Schools designed to minimize architectural barriers to movement.

The true natural history of each of the above technological and process developments is relatively unclear. There is some evidence, however, that they grew from beginnings in the education and rehabilitation of the handicapped, some starting near the turn of the present century.

Not very much is known about optimum educational space for

handicapped children once one moves beyond the accepted rules for eliminating architectural barriers to movement.[12] So, what is in this chapter represents the best judgment of the authors and that of others with whom they have talked or whose ideas they have read.

Research is needed to confirm or reject a great many of the concepts presented here. But until that is done, the ideas in the following chapters are good ones, and they should be used by those responsible for the development of facilities for handicapped children, youth, and adults. The results will be superior to those begun from ground zero or copied from an earlier work which copied an earlier work, and so on into history.

BEHAVIORAL EFFECTS OF ENVIRONMENT

The management of social and academic learning behavior is certainly the domain of the teacher. By *management* is meant initiation, reduction, acceleration, and other forms of controlled manipulation. The environment can support or defeat the teacher if it has significant affects.

The movement of people in certain environments can be influenced by light and color. In an art gallery setting, a light beige room, with all other matters equal, held people longer and with more intensive or dense movement patterns than did a dark brown room. Also, human response to mental and visual tasks appeared to be facilitated by soft and deep colors in the environment.

When tests are given and responded to over a substantial period of time in beautiful and ugly rooms, both those giving the tests and those taking them in the ugly rooms experienced more fatigue, discomfort, monotony, irritability, and feelings of wishes to avoid the room. Photographs received more positive ratings in the beautiful rooms.

There are clearly several ways to increase the probability of eliciting certain human behaviors by changing environmental conditions. Before any great advantage can be taken of that knowledge, however, architects and educators and other professional planners need more research evidence in applied situations that are closer to actual instruction. In the meantime, they will need to rely on intuitive extrapolations from the limited research available and upon their own judgement and experience.

We are in the midst of an extremely important shift in emphasis on the perception and consideration of the critical relationships between a building and its surroundings and the people who use it or are affected by it. The emphasis, here, is on the effect of that relationship.

The effect can be salutory or catastrophic; it can even have a chain reaction over a large area. It can help shape or destroy anything from a neighborhood to a society. This makes architecture, correctly understood and practiced, almost frighteningly important. And it is.

The hardest new lesson is the recognition that a facility used by a live organization is never finished. *It is never finished.* It is, on the contrary, always in a state of adjustment, growth, and restatement. This is what the living process is all about.

"We didn't know the future was coming," is the excuse of fools.

THE LEARNING ENVIRONMENT

We are concerned here about the manner in which children learn and the impact of their physical environment on the effectiveness of that learning experience. We are concerned because *we* create that environment. No one has yet precisely and conclusively defined the characteristics of the space within which children learn most easily and respond most positively. While many questions have been asked and some research has been done, the field has yet to be plowed.

We know that a child's education is made up of everything that happens to him, good and bad, at home and at school. The shaping of the learning environment must hinge on what we intend the child to do, because *he learns from what he does and only from what he does.* Much happens accidentally without forethought or planning. The child can learn sitting under the blue sky in an open field. That is, he can learn effectively if he is comfortable. Since we cannot control the weather, we protect him from it by enclosing space. We cannot afford a teacher for every child, so we gather them together in a teaching-learning place. We try to make it a comfortable place, a friendly place, a child's place, where he can feel secure and safe, free of the tensions that may affect his learning.

The environment within which the child is growing physically, intellectually, and emotionally is an environment that we, the administrator, the teacher, and the architect create: the great teaching machine that we call a school building.

Correction of Learning Deficits

Compare what a normal child does and sees before he enters school at age six with the experiences of most handicapped children. If the child has no mobility he may be out of his home unaccompanied for the first time in his life, set adrift in a strange world. The magnitude of his deficit is challenging, even a little frightening, to an inexperienced teacher.

Handicapped children with poor motor coordination, with impaired senses, with little experience or initiative, start school with much to make up if they are even to reach the level of their peers. Both the teacher and the architect must devise enriching experiences utilizing all of the pupil's senses: visual, auditory, kinesthetic and tactile.

We are concerned about the exceptional child's learning deficits and the ways in which the physical environment may minimize or hopefully eliminate these deficits. In order to learn and to perform effectively, the child should feel good about what he is doing, and secure and assured that he is safe. The handicapped child will often need help, but too much supportive help may lessen his will and his ability to do things for himself. He will withdraw from challenge and become fearful of failure unless we guide him to success experiences. Since handicaps will vary, provision must be made for the supportive help that is a *must*. We need not change the type of typical door knobs because some children may be unable to grasp, but we must modify toilets to provide usable facilities for every child, whatever his handicap.

To maximize the richness of each child's experience, the whole school building indoors and out must be considered and used as a large teaching instrument within which are smaller teaching instruments and teachers who create experiences that will arouse the child's interest and guide him to independent and, finally, spontaneous activity: floors, walls, ceilings, learning spaces, corridors, and toilets are all essential, usable parts of the teaching instrument. All children are first *learners,* second handicapped. Their education must be based on what they can do, not on what they can't, and insure insofar as possible, that everything they do is a success experience. To reinforce this effort, it is imperative to design the teaching instrument carefully. We must shape the learning environment to support the effort of the teacher, but, above all, it must be designed to stimulate and support the effort of the handicapped child. We must not overlook the fact that we can also create, unconsciously or thoughtlessly, an environment that obstructs learning, and makes it difficult and discouraging.

A New View of the Classroom

We are accustomed to thinking of schools in terms of classrooms. For over a hundred years, we have thought of them as self-contained boxes of space strung along a path we called a corridor. Fortunately, the inflexible and confining *classroom* concept is falling apart under the hammering of those who see greater opportunities for educational progress in unencumbered, controllable free space with options. No one will deny that learning is affected by the environment in which it takes place.

To reflect and adequately serve the teacher's needs and the children's needs, we are recognizing that the learning space must be fluid and flexible. The teacher should have the option of adjusting it to suit the teaching task. Unlike the row of self-contained, identical classrooms, it should be capable of responding to change, to innovative thinking that can demonstrate that change is desirable, and to the inevitable future that we cannot yet describe.

The term *classroom* is a concept that may or may not fit well when applied to normal children. We do know, however, that it does not fit well when we apply it to the education of the handicapped. For many years, we have assumed that what is the accepted learning space for normal children must be good learning space for handicapped children, provided that we modify it slightly! Planners of many schools for the handicapped have overlooked the evidence that learning experiences for handicapped children are often different from the learning experiences for normal children; and the problems of the teacher are similarly different, since the learning environment is a reflection of teaching methods and objectives. Learning space for the handicapped must be different. (See Chapters V, VI, VII). The broad range of handicaps and multiple handicaps, often within the same learning groups, forces us to rethink the design of the learning space. We may be sure that children will not be seated in orderly rows facing a teacher and a chalkboard.

Accommodating to Diversity

Some forward looking teachers have been so bold as to ask whether our present systems have the ability to accommodate the broad range of differences found in a typical school for the handicapped. We acknowledge without question that programs must recognize diversity. It follows that space must recognize diversity. To be effective, it must acknowledge that the school environment of handicapped children needs to provide many experiences that are not at all similar to the experiences of normal children. It must try to make up for the deficits caused by limited mobility, limited intelligence, or emotional disturbances. It must recognize that present day schools for normal children are generally dedicated to visual learning. Yet, a significant percentage of the school population is not capable of learning mainly from visual techniques. Handicapped children do not all learn efficiently by seeing and being told, "Do it this way." If their learning problems are not recognized early enough, they may eventually be taught in a school for handicapped children. An alert teacher will determine by which modality the child best receives information and by which modality he most effectively responds. Must he work alone or can he work with others, should he have experience with younger children, with older children, in a small group or a larger group? The teacher must have options—both in the content and design of the learning experience and an option in the learning environment—to choose for the experience.

If we approach the design of learning space for handicapped children and acknowledge that it is different than the problem for normal children; and if we approach it with a fresh, open mind, hopefully the teacher and the architect, in meaningful cooperation, can devise a learning environment more effective and imaginative than any we have yet seen. As Cruickshank and Quay have said, "Few school buildings are conceptualized, designed, and constructed to meet the learning needs of the children for whom the structures were intended." [44]

It is hoped that the discussion which follows will contribute to the ultimate solution of this problem. We must find the kind of intense remediation that will hopefully remove learning deficits and modify behavior patterns to the point of enabling handicapped children to join the mainstream of education at the outset and to remain on a full- or part-time basis in the regular program. We are compelled to re-examine every aspect of the physical environment to insure that it is making its maximum contribution to this goal.

THE TEACHING TASK

The principal accepted objectives of any educational program for handicapped children have as their targets to develop interest in normal attitudes and normal behavior, to develop curiosity about all aspects of the world around them, to encourage the desire to communicate with others, and to stimulate each child to learn more in happy association with other children. But the same can be said for normal children. If the objectives are similar, why the *special* education?

Different Task Requires Different Environment

Because the objectives for both groups have much in common and because education for the handicapped was started long after normal education was an accepted pattern, education of the handicapped and the schools in which it takes place have been considered as modifications of the normal. Provision of the physical environment for the handicapped has been a slightly modified version of the regular school. In some instances, there has been no modification whatsoever. One of the authors once visited a new school for educable and trainable mentally retarded children. The classrooms were the usual boxes of space with regimented rows of desks and chalkboards on two walls, even in the rooms for children who admittedly could never learn to write. It caused one to wonder whether the school was designed for the children or to gratify the parents.

Recognizing that the academic portion of the teaching-learning objectives must include the three R's insofar as the child is capable of learning, we should examine and analyze the other objectives that are peculiar to, and a major part of, the education of the handicapped. These are the more important characteristics and those that will have the greatest impact on the shape of the learning environment. We have reached a point in educational progress at which we must recognize that education of the handicapped child is not *special*, a modification of normal. *It is different*: the teaching task is different and the physical environment must be different.

Accepting the fact that an educational program, in all of its aspects, is concerned with the growth and development of the *whole* child, how must it be different? These differences will be the *shapers* of the learning environment.

Concern for handicapped children forces us to recognize that normal programs must be supplemented to meet their peculiar needs. It is not quite so obvious that these supplementary *shapers* may have even greater impact on preparation for happy, independent living, which, above all, is the major goal for all education.

Illustrations of Differences

Consider the following tabulation as an illustration of the problem. It is not meant to be complete but should help to orient our creative effort to reach more meaningful solutions to the design of physical space. A list of these differences includes the following:

1. Limited mobility means diminished experiences with the world about them. The school must do everything within its power to reduce or eliminate this deficit by enrichment of school experiences.
2. *Interest* must be learned when experiences and curiosity are limited. It must be stimulated by the physical environment and encouraged by success experiences.
3. Instruction in self-care is imperative for many, including feeding and grooming.
4. Instruction in home care is essential.
5. Problems of behavior modification are more severe. Social interaction does not come as naturally. Acceptable social behavior and intercommunication must be developed.
6. The improvement of motor functions, including coordination, equilibrium, and spatial orientation, is essential for most children.
7. Speech, hearing, and physical therapies are often necessary.
8. Development of sensory and perceptual skills, learning by experience, guiding, directing, touching, smelling, tasting, must be emphasized.

9. Normal children learn to play naturally early in life. Many handicapped children must be taught to play.

10. Independence and success in the world of work must focus on the early recognition and development of practical skills related to employability.

11. Preparation for constructive leisure time activities must be developed.

12. A more positive programmed system for recognition and rewards for success experiences should be devised.

13. A program of family education to insure that the learning experiences are reinforced by similar continuing experiences at home must be implemented.

The above list is far from exhaustive. It should be long enough, though, to make it plain that the teaching task for exceptional children is neither more of the same, nor less of the same, nor selected parts of the same. It is *different* in the most profound sense of the term.

INFLUENCE OF BUILDING ON LEARNING

Well-planned buildings facilitate learning. There may be little *hard* research evidence to form a foundation for that statement, but there is a large body of opinion to support it.

When a well-designed school is also well built, the community has acquired an asset of high value and with a long life of service. For that reason, every school needs to be developed with both the present and future in mind. The educational specifications should reflect, first, what the courses of study and the pupils are like now and what they will be like in the years immediately ahead. They should also reflect, however, the educator's best guesses about what demands education will place on the structure when it is twenty to forty years old, and that is more difficult to estimate.

The most desirable futuristic concept is flexibility. Construction now being planned should include the following characteristics if it is to allow excellent special education programs to be incorporated in it one, two, or three decades hence. The school being built now to serve the future's and today's school:

1. Should be able to accommodate children with single handicaps of a more severe degree.
2. Should be adjustable to instruction of parent-child combinations of all ages, from babes in arms and infants and toddlers, to young adults with their mothers and fathers.
3. Should be suitable for children who have two or more handicapping conditions.
4. Should be able to accommodate increased differentiation of staffing, with teams of teachers, aides, and assistants.
5. Should be able to adjust to the probability that there will be more handicapped children assigned to regular schools and fewer to special schools in the next several years.

CHAPTER V

EXCEPTIONAL CHILDREN WHO REQUIRE SPECIAL EDUCATION

THIS SECTION DEALS with many of the characteristics of exceptional children. Those characteristics which have particularly high relevance to education have been chosen for emphasis.

First, there is an overview of the educational setting, the nature of the children, and the broad kinds of educational adaptations they require. That is followed by more detailed statements about each of the generally recognized groups of exceptional children who need special education.

Standard Terminology [134] defines exceptional children as follows:

> . . . children who, because of certain atypical characteristics, have been identified by professionally qualified personnel as requiring special educational planning and services, whether or not such services are available. In general, the term *exceptional children* considers exceptionality on the basis of (a) physical handicap, (b) emotional and/or social handicap, and (c) measurable exceptionality in mental ability (i.e. mentally gifted and mentally retarded). Some exceptional children have more than one type of exceptionality.

Another frequently used definition is that by Kirk [98] which reads:

> . . . the child who deviates from the average or normal child (1) in mental characteristics, (2) in sensory abilities, (3) in neuromuscular or physical characteristics, (4) in social or emotional behavior, (5) in communication abilities, or (6) in multiple handicaps to such an extent that he requires a modification of school practices or special education services in order to develop to his maximum capacity.

Clearly, there is no essential conflict between these two definitions. Both refer to a *need* for "special education planning and services" or "modification of school practices or special educational services" as the objective criterion which sorts out exceptional children, educationally speaking, from exceptional children, in general, some of whom have exceptionalities which are not those which call for special education. This is a point, then, at which a definition of special education is needed.

The Standard Terminology [134] defines special education as follows:

> . . . education provisions which are different from or in addition to those provided in the usual school program and are provided for exceptional pupils by specially qualified personnel. Special education may be provided in special classes on a full-time or part-time basis; outside the school plant in the pupil's home, hospital, a sanatorium, or a convalescent home; or in other appropriate settings.

That rather general definition needs to be given more body if it is to give guidance in the design of schools and schooling. In what follows, we intend to supply part of the needed substance by describing what it is that special educators do as they pursue their various specialties. It is not our intent to present a training manual for the preparation of special educators. Instead, we have concentrated more on job description information, the kind of information which architects, educational administrators, and board of education members need.

We have organized the material on exceptional children under a series of headings, as follows:

1. Speech Handicapped Children and Youth.
2. Mentally Retarded Children and Youth.
3. Gifted and Talented Children and Youth.
4. Visually Handicapped Children and Youth.
5. Children and Youth with Hearing Handicaps.
6. Children and Youth with Learning Disabilities.
7. Children and Youth who are Crippled, Neurologically Impaired, or Health Impaired.
8. Children and Youth with Developmental Disabilities.

We recognize that those groupings are not necessarily mutually exclusive. Also, they are not necessarily the groupings common to all state special education laws or regulations. However, we do find that the groupings are very suitable for this book's purposes, and that has been verified by a number of educators who reviewed the material in manuscript form.

For each of the above headings, we have tried to supply information on a number of topics. These cover definitions, objectives of education, incidence and prevalence, types and degrees of handicaps, typical school settings, and special procedures for instruction. Obviously, all of these items do not apply under each heading, and some headings call for other data. But these items do reflect the general organizational pattern for what follows.

SPEECH HANDICAPPED CHILDREN AND YOUTH

Definition

Speech handicapped children are those whose speech draws unfavorable attention to itself, because it is difficult to understand, unpleasant sounding, or otherwise not near enough to accepted standards. Three or four out of every one hundred children usually are speech handicapped.

Types

Fortunately, the most common and most prevalent speech defects are also the ones which can be corrected most successfully. These are called articulation defects, and they include sound substitutions, omissions, distortions and additions.

Therapy with articulation defects and with other, more complex speech handicaps is the responsibility of the speech clinician in the schools. These more involved conditions include stuttering, voice disorders, delayed speech, and speech problems associated with various physical handicaps. The latter, for example, include speech handicaps related to defective hearing, cleft palate and cleft lip, and cerebral palsy.

School Settings

Typically, the speech clinician talks with kindergarten and primary grade children, picks out those who need help with their speech, and establishes procedures for correcting the difficulties. Much therapy is done on a one-to-one or very small group basis. The clinician and the regular classroom teacher agree on schedules that allow speech handicapped children to leave their classmates for ten to twenty minute periods, and to go to the speech correctionist's headquarters for corrective lessons once or twice a week. Case loads for this kind of work are usually in the range of 90 to 110 pupils per week for one clinician, though more advanced professional standards would call for a reduction in that number.

The clinician usually has a headquarters area or room with a central location. The supplies and equipment needed for individual therapy are kept there and make for efficiency in use and maintenance.

Speech clinicians are often itinerant, giving service to several schools. There appears to be an advantage to assign schools on a *family of schools* basis. That means that the same clinician would serve a high school, the junior high schools or middle schools which send pupils to that high school, and the elementary schools, whose pupils, in turn, flow to the same middle or junior high schools. To the extent that it can be done, it helps to assure continuity in the professional management of the youngsters who have speech problems, especially those which call for long-term therapy.

Objectives and Procedures

More and more, speech clinicians are playing an added role with children in the early childhood years. Speech clinicians are teaming with kindergarten and first and second grade teachers in conducting speech improvement activities. A large proportion of four to eight-year-olds have not yet learned to articulate certain sounds correctly. Their speech is still developing. The clinician helps the teacher to use workbooks, recordings, story telling, sound games, and guided play to encourage youngsters to improve their still faulty articulation. That work is carried on cooperatively between the clinician and the teacher as part of the regular language arts activities of the kindergarten-primary period. Such speech improvement instruction* moves children in an orderly way through the speech maturation sequence and helps to prevent defective articulation in later years.

Speech clinicians also furnish consultation to upper grade and high school teachers who have children with speech defects in their classes. The speech correctionist helps teachers to know how to minimize speech problems for pupils who stutter, how to assure that children

---

*An example is found in the *Best Speech Series,* workbooks for regular class teachers or parents to use with children under the guidance of a speech clinician. (Stanwix House. Inc., Pittsburgh, Pa.)

who have hearing losses are able to understand the teacher and other pupils, and how to deal with other such individual cases so as to avert problems.

The speech clinician is as much a counselor as a correctionist in the case of many children. There are frequent occasions, too, for conferences with parents. In many instances, speech clinicians guide parents in how to improve their children's speech through planned home activities.

Speech clinicians can often be very helpful in the design of instructional facilities. Their professional training tends to assure that they can specify clearly what activities they will be carrying out in the space used as an headquarters and in the other spaces where they will be joining with other teachers for certain kinds of instruction.

Speech clinicians also work in residential schools, day schools, hospitals, child development centers, rehabilitation centers, and clinics. In a few instances, such locales are concerned only with persons with defective speech. More often, they are facilities which take care of mentally retarded, hearing handicapped, or other exceptional children whose conditions frequently have speech defects associated with them. In the latter instances, the work of the speech therapist tends to be much more oriented to individual correction. However, there are also group developmental classes for mentally retarded pupils similar to those speech clinicians carry on in team work with regular class teachers.

MENTALLY RETARDED CHILDREN AND YOUTH

Definition

Special education for mentally retarded pupils has many faces and various names. It can be seen in residential schools, in public or private schools, in separate day schools, and integrated in regular elementary and secondary schools. Among its many names are Adaptive Education, Developmental Training, Orthogenic Education, and Occupational Education, in addition to the most widely used term, Special Education for the Mentally Retarded. But schooling for mentally retarded children has certain common characteristics despite its many forms and titles.

First, all education for mentally retarded children is slower paced than for children in general. Second, all education for mentally retarded pupils has less complex objectives than for other children. As an example of the first, it may well take the most able retarded pupil until the age of sixteen or eighteen to learn to read at fifth or sixth grade level. As an example of the second, learning to read at the fifth or sixth grade level (which allows reading most advertisements and newspapers) may be the highest objective for certain retarded pupils. There will be other retarded pupils for whom recognizing signs like STOP and DANGER may be the highest attainable reading objectives, and they may take years to learn those important words.

Mentally retarded children, like other children, increase in learning ability as they grow older. Their learning potentials are higher in the late teens than they are in earlier years. Schooling, however slowly paced, can have significant values for retarded persons in the years from age eighteen to twenty-one.

It is not possible to predict accurately just what or how much an individual mentally retarded child will prove capable of learning. So, teachers are constantly helping retarded pupils to stretch beyond their current achievements. For the most retarded, learning to walk or to feed one's self can make a monumental difference over the years in that individual's degree of self-fulfillment and in the degree of help needed from others. For the least retarded, increasing reading skill from fifth to seventh grade level or graduating from grocery bagging to shelf inventorying and stocking are giant educational and vocational steps. While they might take two or three years of instruction, they make decades of difference in the level of self-maintenance throughout adult life.

Types

Mentally retarded persons make up about 3 percent of the total population. They are usually divided into three levels for educational purposes. The group called the *educable mentally retarded* is the most capable, so far as school learning is concerned. By the time individuals in this group are eighteen to twenty-one years old, most can acquire academic skills up to the sixth grade standard or higher, which means they have adequate literacy for most recreational, job, and personal requirements. When well-taught, they disappear into society as adults who are perfectly capable of self-maintenance and good citizenship under normal conditions. This is also the largest group of the mentally retarded, probably accounting for approximately two thirds of all the mentally retarded.

Pupils in the next level of mental retardation are called *trainable mentally retarded*. They comprise about one fourth of the children and youth population who are mentally retarded. Instructional programs for trainable retarded persons emphasize learning to talk, to dress, to work in a sheltered setting, to enjoy music and both spectator and participating games, and to participate effectively in ordinary family and group social activities.

When educators first began to use the terms *educable* and *trainable* to distinguish levels of retardation, it was to convey the idea that the educable group could achieve literacy and learn, at an elementary level, to use reading and numbers as tools for personal, vocational, and social advantage. Trainable retarded persons were presumed to be unable to attain functional literacy. Instead, they were to be taught only to recognize, as indicated earlier, survival symbols like stop signs, danger signs, and the like, so far as reading was concerned.

Approximately twenty-five years ago, public schools in a few places began to organize instruction for trainable retarded pupils. The separation between them and educable retarded pupils was quite distinct. The intelligence quotient demarkations tended to be as follows:

Educable Mentally Retarded	IQ	50 to 75
Trainable Mentally Retarded	IQ	30 to 49
Untrainable and Uneducable Mentally Retarded	IQ	0 to 29

It was found, over a period of time, that while intelligence tests had important values, they were not precise or accurate enough to justify placing so much dependence upon them as was being done. It is still true that intelligence quotients are widely used. But a growing tendency is to consider an intelligence quotient as supplying an estimate of intelligence rather than an exact measure. Also, and most important, the estimate provided by the intelligence quotient is usually considered (a) a minimal estimate, (b) a measure of current functioning intelligence, and (c) capable of being improved or increased to some extent through instruction. In short, the point of view that intelligence itself can be influenced by instruction has recently gained a great deal of currency.

Procedures for Teaching

One practical result is that dynamic instructional approaches are more common. Emphasis is on potentialities rather than limitations. Instead of assuming that a measured IQ of 20 is *prima facie* evidence that a pupil cannot be trained or educated, serious efforts are now made to produce added development and a more rapid pace of development through instruction. It is only after a reasonable period of deliberate and planned teaching that it is possible to be more definite about the actual degree of retardation present in a pupil. And it is increasingly clear that almost no one is completely untrainable and uneducable.

So, schools and teachers are moving toward a *zero reject* posture with regard to mentally retarded individuals, a posture in which instruction at some level and of some potentially useful character is begun in the early childhood years with all apparently retarded pupils, and continued until age twenty-one or until the pupil makes a move from the school to independence in the community. The latter, of course, is the main goal, and it can be achieved for the great majority of retarded persons. But even instruction which attempts and reaches such a limited goal as teaching a profoundly retarded person to cooperate with an attendant while being fed is highly valued. It is worthwhile both for the degree of communication and self-fulfillment of the retarded person and the importance for society, in that the retarded person is somewhat more self-reliant and less costly to maintain.

The role of the teacher with retarded pupils is to bring them to the highest levels of education possible. Teachers of retarded pupils are encouraged to design their instruction to stretch their pupils rather than to simply accept their retardation as a completely unalterable limitation.

School Settings

Education for retarded pupils of all levels takes place most commonly in self-contained special classes in regular elementary and secondary schools. For educable retarded pupils there is a noticeable trend toward inclusion with all other children in regular class groups by bringing special education to them there. A less common, but still present arrangement, is the special day school for mentally retarded pupils.

More severely involved mentally retarded children, especially those with multiple handicaps, tend to find their way to residential schools, either state or private.

In public schools, a resource room approach is also quite frequently used. It is found at both elementary and secondary school levels in many school districts.

Objectives

Specialists in the education of mentally retarded students concur that the overarching goal should be effective, independent living. The achievement of that goal is expected as a matter of course for nonhandicapped pupils. For those who are mentally retarded it is a much less certain attainment. For many retarded pupils it is achieved only through an arduous struggle to learn skills and understandings which are acquired much more easily by their more intelligent brothers and sisters. So it is not surprising that typical instructional objectives focus on:

1. Skills of safe living at home and in the community.
2. Habituating cleanliness and related good health habits.
3. Understandings and skills basic to earning a living.
4. Getting along with other people socially and at work.
5. Attaining reading and writing, literacy, and basic oral communication skills.
6. Using social technology such as transportation systems, the mails, banks, and government agencies.
7. Using recreational facilities and understanding nature.
8. Housekeeping and household management, including rents, mortgages, installment buying and other purchasing, and family and personal financial planning.

Family, social, and civic competencies are deliberately taught, rather than allowing them to develop through incidental learning as they do for most people. It is of paramount importance that pupils learn acceptable work habits and salable skills so they may maintain themselves in competitive employment in adulthood.

If one were to try to encompass the kinds of specific educational objectives which loom highest for the teacher of mentally retarded pupils, they could probably be classed in three groups. Teaching aimed at:

1. Sound personal and emotional adjustment.
2. Effective social living (social adjustment).
3. Self-maintenance (economic adjustment).

Mentally retarded individuals who have less potential have simpler educational objectives. The targets for trainable mentally retarded children and youth are just as realistic, and they are just as difficult to achieve, even though they are at a level with less promise of independent functioning. Objectives are frequently stated as follows:

1. To attain self-management to the degree that supervising and support services are required only occasionally under conditions of change or stress.
2. To acquire skills and understandings which motivate socially useful and continued productive work, usually under sheltered workshop or similarly supervised conditions.
3. To gain self-confidence, self-esteem, and related personal feelings of worth.
4. To achieve speaking and listening competency sufficient to engage in functional and pleasurable communication.

It is clear that the above objectives emphasize the kinds of attainments needed to live and work in sheltered environments. Of course, it is intended that every effort will be made to carry the retarded pupils beyond those objectives if that is possible. Teachers of mentally retarded pupils proceed one step at a time, and the steps are often small ones. But they are constantly seeking ways to take their students further. Every time an objective is attained, a new one is set a little beyond the one just reached. Thus, it is sometimes found that the boy or girl who, at age fifteen or sixteen, was operating within trainable retarded ranges can, by the age of nineteen or twenty, be able to function in the educable retarded range.

The same principle holds true for work with children who, at the outset, appear most profoundly retarded. Teachers and their helpers; parents and families; institutional workers, all who are in contact with profoundly retarded persons, are actively conducting deliberate stimulation activities with them. These include physical movement, talking, music, changes in the visual environment, all the activities calculated to help initiate and carry on motor, cognitive, and affective development. Now, such instruction frequently begins at home with infants as soon as retardation is suspected. And many older, profoundly retarded persons who have not had the benefit of such attention are beginning to receive it in the hope of remedying the deficits which have accumulated through neglect.

Teachers of retarded persons carry out a dynamic program of instruction to produce conditions for maximum development. Each part of the curriculum is linked to either social, personal, or occupational competence.

GIFTED AND TALENTED CHILDREN AND YOUTH

Definitions, Incidence and Prevalence

The term *gifted* refers, in this context, to pupils with unusually high learning potential. Generally it includes youngsters with quite high intelligence quotients, as high as 130 and upwards. They make up approximately 3 or 4 percent of all children and youth and they have the potential for excellent achievement at the highest levels of formal education in professional and graduate schools.

The expression *talented* is meant to refer to children and youth who reveal unusual potentialities for accomplished performance and composition in music, for sculpture and painting, and for literature, for the dance, and for the theatre.

Both gifted and talented pupils may also be creative, that is, inventive and very capable of turning the commonplace into the unusual in useful and pleasing ways.

Many handicapped children are also either gifted, talented, or both. Many possess great creativity. Thus the schools they attend need to be designed and equipped, in staff and materials, to help develop pupils' gifts, talents, and creative potentials.

The U.S. Office of Education's Bureau for the Education of the

Handicapped has federal responsibility for the education of the gifted. At the state level, the same assignment has often been given to the Division of Special Education in the State Education Agency. Those offices have resources, both in terms of publications and staff consultants, of real value to those planning schools for exceptional children of all kinds.

Objectives and School Settings

The programs for gifted and talented children in the United States tend to be both vertical and horizontal extensions of regular school programs. That means accelerated regular programs, or more breadth to regular programs, or both. Those approaches certainly have value, for children are encouraged to learn more and to learn faster, and both are advantageous.

As of this time, however, we have not been able to detect differences of any substantial kind which are called for in school design or construction that would enhance the interface between the gifted pupil and the teacher. It is of fundamental importance, however, that programs for gifted and talented pupils be housed so as to be fully accessible to students who have mobility problems. If not, many handicapped pupils will be denied scholarly and artistic colleagueship with their age peers of like minds and talents.

VISUALLY HANDICAPPED CHILDREN AND YOUTH

Objectives

The education of visually handicapped children is the same as that for their seeing brothers and sisters, with three exceptions. Added to regular education, visually handicapped students need:

1. To be taught to control their environment. That means to be mobile; that is, to walk out doors, to use public transportation, to move about in houses and buildings and places of business, and to use amenities. It also means to acquire and use mental maps and checklists for dressing, to use thermostats and air conditioners, to store valuable papers, and to do the multitude of other activities necessary to live independently but without sufficient vision for seeing all the things which others do.

2. To be taught concepts and understandings and skills which are not feasible for visually handicapped persons to learn in the usual ways. An example applicable to totally blind persons would be the concept of color and the understandings related to it. The blue sky, the green meadow—the very idea of a color, to say nothing of the emotional toning which accompanies such terms as yellow streak, red flag, deep purple—these cannot be perceived directly; they must be painstakingly taught by indirection. With respect to reading, the use of Braille for blind persons and the use of enlarged type for partially seeing persons are examples of approaching the development of literacy in special ways.

3. To be taught to make full use of any vision the pupil may have. There are relatively few children who have no vision at all. Even if there remains only the ability to distinguish generally between light and dark, or only vague shapes, or only glimmering tunnel vision, it is possible to teach the visually handicapped person to make maximum use of that residual vision in relation to items one and two above. Without special teaching and maintenance activities, the use of residual vision tends to decrease; with special training and practice, the use of even a limited degree of visual perception can be a major asset.

Thus, special education for visually limited persons derives from the basic three considerations noted above. The school setting, the instructional materials, the specialized staff, and any curricular adaptations are there to effect the *normalization* of visually handicapped persons. The objective is to help them acquire as much freedom as possible for independent living.

It is important to keep in mind, of course, that visually handicapped persons are just as liable, or more liable, to all other kinds of handicapping conditions, too. Some visually handicapped persons are mentally retarded, some are crippled, some are deaf, and so on. Where those or other combinations of handicaps occur, it is necessary to develop additional special accommodations.

As indicated earlier, the purposes to be accomplished in educating visually handicapped pupils include all those for nonhandicapped individuals plus certain additions which make up the special part of their education. That point of view has been put into similar words by many leaders in the special education of visually handicapped.

> One of the most consistent aims, as reflected throughout our history in the education of blind children, has been that blind children, within the limits of their abilities and problems common to all children, should be able to pursue the same curriculum as that provided sighted children.[1]
> The school program should be planned to meet the needs of each individual child and be directed toward guiding him toward well adjusted adulthood in our democratic society.[141]
> The most important factor in increasing the blind child's ability to gain experience is his own ability to get about and secure it by himself.
> For the blind child, developing mobility, orientation, and effective skills for living is something like the "Kingdom of God." It should be sought first and other things can be added unto it.
> The goal of programs of mobility and orientation for blind children is an optimum degree of independent functioning by the individual.
> The educational program for the visually limited must also emphasize the development of meaningful concepts.
> Several important points about reading and writing in braille should be stressed.
> It has frequently been said that the content and methods of instruction for both the blind and the partially seeing are the same as those for seeing children, and that only the media differ—braille, audio and tactual aids, and large type. In general, this is true.[14]
> Education must work at giving the blind child a knowledge of the realities around him, the confidence to cope with these realities, and the feeling that he is recognized and accepted as an individual in his own right.[104, 105]
> As with all atypical children, the visually handicapped child's basic needs and the goals for his education are not different from those of the ordinary child.[98]

Definitions and Types

Educators generally now refer to visually handicapped pupils as either:

1. Blind, meaning those who cannot learn to read print through use of their eyes, and must learn to read tactually by braille.
2. Visually impaired, meaning those who can learn to read print, but must have extraordinary visual help to do so, usually by directly increased size of print or by magnification by special lenses.

Obviously, these are individuals whose vision cannot be corrected to normal or near normal by the usual kinds of spectacles or even with the most powerful manageable magnifications and related corrections.

Incidence and Prevalence

So far as the prevalence of blind and visually handicapped school age groups is concerned, estimates vary. Conservatively, it may be considered that one out of every 3,000 pupils in a school district can be expected to be blind, and that one out of every 750 pupils will classify as visually impaired. The conditions which cause visual handicaps occur more frequently when children have poor health care, poor nutrition, and where there are many safety hazards. Thus, certain communities can be expected to have higher or lower prevalence of visual handicaps, depending on the factors just mentioned. Also, there is a tendency for parents with visually handicapped children to move into communities which are known for high quality special education, rehabilitation, and medical services. The same is true for other handicapping conditions. Such considerations make it advisable for each school district to develop its own data on incidence and prevalence for facilities' planning purposes.

Settings for Education

In America today visually handicapped pupils are taught in the following settings:

1. Special residential schools.
2. Special day schools.
3. Special classes in wings of regular schools.
4. Special classes centrally located in regular schools.
5. Part-time in special classes or resource rooms and part-time in regular classes.
6. Full-time in regular classes with support personnel aiding the regular teacher.
7. Combinations of the above (i.e. special residential or day schools, but part-time attendance at a nearby regular elementary or high school).

It is possible for visually handicapped pupils, either blind or visually impaired, to receive a sound education in any of the above settings.

There are noticeable trends, however. One major trend is to conduct the special education of visually handicapped pupils in regular classes from the very outset, bringing to the regular teachers and the visually handicapped children whatever special education is needed. A second major trend is for special residential and day schools to tool up to work mainly with visually handicapped pupils who, for a variety of reasons, present even more complex educational problems than usual.

These might include the complications of deafness and visual handicaps, severe crippling conditions coupled with visual handicaps, and the like. The special residential or day school tries in such cases to be a short-term setting, bringing intensive staff work to bear on whatever problems prevent the pupil from attending a regular school.

The two trends just mentioned apply to both blind and visually impaired pupils. In fact, as suggested earlier, the previous sharp distinction between the two groups, a distinction based on visual acuity and related medical criteria, has given way to a graduation of descriptive distinctions based on what educational procedures and materials are used.

A third noticeable trend is earlier education. Blind or visually impaired children are now more often being detected in very early life. Stimulation procedures can be used with babies by their parents, under educational supervision, to bring into play the senses of touch, smell, hearing, and motion in ways that help compensate for absence or limitation of vision. Concurrently, the early use of vision aids acclimates children to using what vision they have. Schooling at home, in nurseries, and in combinations is growing. In Pennsylvania, for example, the state supports education for blind children beginning at age two. States differ in this kind of provision; it is essential to thoughtful school design that the planners be aware of such state regulations and trends.

Professionally prepared teachers of visually handicapped pupils may operate in any of several roles, or may shift from one role to another. The five major roles are commonly defined as follows:[93]

CONDUCTING A FULL-TIME SPECIAL CLASS: Here the teacher may be in charge of a class in a special residential school, a special day school, a wing of a regular elementary or secondary school, or a room within such a school. The actual work of the teacher will be conditioned by where the special class is located, of course. But the central factor in any case is that the teacher has full responsibility for instructing a group of seven to nine pupils in practically all components of the curriculum. Some of the children may from time to time go to other teachers for curricular areas like music or physical education, but no youngster would have more than one fourth of his formal instruction outside the full-time special class.

CONDUCTING A COOPERATIVE SPECIAL CLASS: Here the teacher is working in a regular elementary or secondary school, with the special classroom situated either in a wing of the building or among regular classes. The crucial factors in defining a *cooperative* special class are (a) that the pupils be on the report roll of the special teachers but (b) that they spend three fourths or more of their time in regular classes with regular teachers. It is apparent that the special class teacher in this setting has full responsibility for only a minor fraction of the curriculum. At the same time, the special education teacher helps regular class teachers with instructional materials, lesson planning, curricular adaptations, and pupil assessment for the visually handicapped pupils on the cooperative class roll. The pupils are scattered into various regular classes during the day. The special education teacher does intensive tutoring with the visually handicapped pupils when their individualized schedules bring them to the special education class. The schedules are made up by the special education teacher with the cooperation of the regular class teachers and the principal.

Often, the special teacher gives advice, provides tutoring help, and does team teaching with regular class teachers of children who may not have vision limitations but who are, according to their regular class teachers, in need of special help. That kind of activity marks a recent departure from a pattern which had previously required special education teachers to deal exclusively with children who had met formal entrance requirements and who were classified as being eligible for special education.

It is increasingly common practice for regular and special teachers to agree to work together for a time with a pupil who is not getting along well. Sometimes they determine that the youngster does need some form of special education, and they arrange to have it provided.

At other times, they find it is a transient condition which their joint efforts can quickly ameliorate or eliminate.

CONDUCTING A RESOURCE ROOM: It is difficult to differentiate between a resource room and the previously described cooperative special class, except on the basis of what may appear to be a technicality. In the cooperative special class, the visually handicapped pupils are enrolled on the class register of the special education teacher. In the resource room pattern, the pupils are on the rolls of their regular class teachers. Otherwise, the two might be indistinguishable.

But the seeming technicality is much more than that. It defines where the pupils belong, which teachers have major responsibility for them, and with which kind of education, regular or special, they are chiefly identified. In the case of the resource room, there are fewer psychological and social barriers to full integration.

CONDUCTING AN ITINERANT TEACHER PLAN: In England, this would be classed as a peripatetic teacher scheme. The blind or partially seeing pupils spend most of their school days in regular classes. They receive special instruction individually or in small groups from specialist teachers who travel among two or more schools and who devote the majority of their time to instruction.

CONDUCTING A TEACHER-CONSULTANT PLAN: This arrangement is the same as the itinerant teacher plan with one exception. The teacher-consultant gives at least 50 percent of the day to the selection and distribution of instructional aids, advisement of regular class teachers, and the supervision of other professional activities which do not involve direct instruction of pupils. In both the itinerant and teacher-consultant plans, there is the necessity for a central headquarters space for office, storage, planning, and related activities, as well as a need for suitable space in each school in which to work when there.

Mobility Instruction

The mobility instructor is a recently emerged specialty. The term *mobility* may, if taken literally, be too limiting as a description of what is involved. More appropriately, the work of this specialist can be considered as helping the visually handicapped person gain control over the environment despite the handicaps of limited or no vision.

That calls for learning to travel, of course. But it also calls for learning how to manage alone in unfamiliar hotel rooms, or for example, how to manipulate all the countless, visually oriented controls on the gadgets we use in daily living.

Some mobility skills are required in the very early years. Systematic instruction, including using sounds, touch, temperature, and movement sensations for cues, begins when the youngster starts formal schooling, usually between the ages of two and five. In this context, the broadened meaning of this instructional aspect is conveyed by using the phrase *orientation and mobility* to categorize it.

The number of orientation and mobility instructors needed, and the amount of time to be devoted to it in the day-to-day work of special and regular class teachers, too, can be determined with reference to two factors. First is the number of visually handicapped pupils to be provided with instruction. If there are only a few, a part-time orientation and mobility instructor may suffice. The second factor is the nature of the handicapping condition. Pupils with some useful vision call for instruction somewhat different from pupils without it. Multiple handicaps complicate the matter and require more time.

The instructor needs a headquarters area plus room for equipment and materials storage. In addition, indoor and outdoor training areas are required. Attention should be given to the variety of settings in which pupils must acquire coping skills and the varying circumstances (i.e. weather conditions, traffic flow, emergencies) under which the skills may need to be correctly applied. The school plant, its site and surroundings, can often be used for those purposes more effectively if appropriate forethought is given during the planning stages.

Procedures for Teaching

It has been estimated that 85 percent of educational experiences and materials are largely visual. Pupils who cannot see or have very limited vision would be at a serious disadvantage unless there were ways to use hearing, touch, smell, and taste to perceive those materials and to gain those experiences.

If it is assumed that individualized instruction is available, the question still remains as to how that instruction is carried out. The following is a summary of what means teachers use to make the required adaptations.

REAL OBJECTS AND MODELS OF OBJECTS are handled by the pupils, and explanations are given that relate them to actual size, use, and location. This is referred to as the use of tangible materials to employ concreteness in teaching.

ACTIVITY, ordinarily encouraged in sighted children by visually attactive things, is deliberately fostered by the use of other senses to stimulate the visually handicapped youngsters to explore their environment, to acquire mental maps of it, and to move through the stages of orientation, mobility, and environment management.

RESIDUAL VISION, no matter how little there is, is put to maximum use. Systematic visual perception training programs are applied and linked to auditory and tactual aids.

BRAILLE, a system of touch reading based on embossed characters, is taught to pupils who have too little vision for the use of *enlarged ink print* books or *magnifiers* with regular print materials. *Braille writing* is also taught as a procedure for taking notes by hand or for preparing materials on a braille typewriter.

TYPING ON STANDARD MACHINES has largely replaced handwriting as a skill, beginning in the early school grades. Listening skills are taught systematically, adding to and enriching those which are acquired incidentally. Natural sounds and the noises of civilization are included. Special attention is given to learning to use tapes and talking books and to note nuances of meaning conveyed by tone or voice.

MATHEMATICAL SKILLS are taught in the usual ways, but there is much more use of tangible materials for such concepts as volume, area, and angles. Use of the abacus and electrical computers is stressed.

FACTORS OF LIGHT AND SOUND are especially important. Glare which can be tolerated by persons of normal vision can render the partially seeing person helpless to use what vision he has. Thus chalkboards, furniture, and wall surfaces, for example, call for special considerations.

NEW TECHNICAL AIDS are always on the horizon. To optimize learning, the visually handicapped person needs to hear as well as possible when engaged in ordinary listening and when using records and recorders. Acoustic treatment of more than ordinary quality is thus advisable. The Optacon is a print-scanning device which reproduces letters as finger tip vibratory images. Light beam scanners for travel using the lasar principle are being developed. Compressed speech listening-training allows comprehension of recorded voices at rates comparable to print reading up to 275 words per minute. These could be in widespread use soon, as could others now in experimental stages.

CHILDREN AND YOUTH WITH HEARING HANDICAPS

School Settings

There are similarities in the way schools are organized to supply education for hearing-handicapped pupils and for visually handicapped pupils in the United States, Canada, England, and other countries. There are also likenesses in the way educational factors have come to take precedence over medical approaches in defining auditory handicaps.

Children who are deaf or hard-of-hearing are being educated in:
1. Special residential schools.
2. Special day schools.
3. Special classes in wings of regular elementary or secondary schools.
4. Special classes placed among other classes in regular elementary or secondary schools.
5. Resource or cooperative class arrangements with pupils attending a large part of each day in regular classes on regular schedules.
6. Regular classes with special education brought to them by specialists who work with the exceptional pupils and their regular teachers.

The education of children with hearing handicaps is the same as that for all children with two exceptions. First, the hearing handicapped pupils must learn to live as self-fulfilled and effective citizens without being able to hear the sounds of the world or hearing them in a dim and distorted way. Second, the hearing handicapped pupils must learn language in special and often roundabout ways rather than acquire language through incidental learning as hearing children do.

Both of these are important problems. But the second is by far the most difficult to manage.

If confronted with the imaginary but stark choice of being born blind or being born deaf, most nonhandicapped adults would probably elect to be born deaf. Sophisticated special educators would tend to take the other alternative. They realize that the absence of hearing from infancy carries with it the failure to acquire language in the normal way. And they know that it can be the most devastating of handicaps.

There is a growing movement in the United States, Canada, and England to include hearing impaired pupils in regular schools. This mainstreaming approach requires the collection of specialized staff, equipment, and materials to support regular class teachers.

At the same time, there are widespread efforts to begin educational contacts with hearing impaired children and their parents at earlier ages. School districts are sending teachers to the homes of deaf infants to demonstrate to mothers and fathers how to stimulate communication. Residential schools are admitting two-to three-year-old toddlers and their mothers for a week or two in the summer to live in with the children and to help in the transition of learning how to continue the children's training when they are at home each weekend during the school year.

The role of the special day school or special residential school for hearing impaired pupils is changing. The most noteworthy directions of change are:

1. Children are being admitted at earlier ages, as young as two or three years, as day or residential pupils.
2. Parents are much more in the scene, and some plans include them as volunteers to help teachers at the schools as well as advising them on ways to aid their children at home.
3. More attention is being given to cooperative arrangements with regular schools which allow pupils to spend increasing portions of their time there and which eventually lead to transfer.
4. Residential schools in particular and special day schools to some extent enroll more multiply handicapped pupils, and modify their programs and facilities to fit the need. (As an example, one well established residential school is now in the

process of installing elevators and ramps to accommodate crippled, deaf pupils who would earlier not have been admitted to the school.)

Objectives

The overriding emphasis in educating children with hearing handicaps is the development of language and communication. Without that help, it is known that the children would remain educationally disabled all of their lives. Therefore, it should come as no surprise that statements of objectives tend to emphasize language and communications.

> Ideally the *hard-of-hearing* child should attend a regular school and, with supplementary help, be able to compete adequately with his classmates.
>
> It is the goal of every educator, whether he be teaching a normal child or a handicapped one, that the techniques used meet the needs of the individual child.
>
> 1. Deaf children can learn to understand language through the multisensory approach (vision, touch, kinesthetics, and hearing).
> 2. They can comprehend language from lipreading, the utilization of residual hearing, and reading.
> 3. They can learn to express language through speech and writing.
> 4. They can learn academic subject matter through our English language.[16]
>
> Every hearing impaired child should be taught to make as much use of his residual hearing as possible at an early date.
>
> Ability by the hearing impaired to speech read and speak are skills second in importance only to language and an education.[17]
>
> In the classrooms of Gallaudet College, oral speech, finger spelling, and signs are used all at the same time in hope that the students may acquire knowledge by whichever means they can grasp more readily.[23]

The above objectives are implemented through the use of vision and residual hearing. Special methods of communication training are used to foster language development, speech reading and auditory training, reading, and in the teaching of other school subjects.

Procedures for Teaching

By the time hearing impaired persons who need special education become adults, they are usually able to make use of speech reading, sign, oral speech, writing, and finger spelling (by the manual alphabet) in some combination. Some are more expert in oral and others in manual modalities.

Three general approaches to teaching hearing impaired pupils are widely recognized. Within each of these general approaches more specific procedures are sometimes identified.

1. Oral Method. Only oral speech, speech reading, the use of residual hearing, and ordinary reading and writing are used. Use of the manual alphabet and sign is discouraged.
2. Combined Method. The oral method is taught jointly with the use of the manual alphabet to spell out what is being communicated.
3. Simultaneous Method. This method employs essentially the combined method but encourages the use of sign as well as finger spelling and uses the latter mainly to make visible what cannot be conveyed adequately by sign. This method, augmented by any other useful sound or visual cues, is sometimes called *total communication*.

There is a history of controversy among educators regarding which of the above approaches is best. That controversy continues in some quarters, but it is diminishing in its influence, if not its heat. There is powerful evidence now that the chief focus must be on helping the pupil, at the earliest age possible, to acquire some form of language usable for communication. Once that is accomplished, it is possible to build a variety of communication procedures upon that foundation.

Definitions and Types

The expression *hearing impaired* has considerable acceptance when used to described a person who requires special education because of some limitation in hearing. Broadly speaking, hearing impaired children form two groups for educational purposes.

The least prevalent group, close to one in one thousand, has hearing deficiencies so severe that, for most practical purposes, hearing is unattainable even with the best of hearing aids. If unable to hear from the first year of life, these children do not know about sounds at all. Also, not being able to hear, they gain no idea about communication through ordinary spoken language. Thus, their chief educational problem is not one of speech, but rather, a much more fundamental one, language. The very existence of oral and audible language must be painstakingly taught, along with language expression through speech. These children are educationally deaf.

The second group, perhaps one in two hundred in prevalence, does acquire language and speech through its own hearing. But these children do so with much difficulty, and the result is imperfect. These children find hearing aids useful. But even with the best of aids, their hearing remains far from normal in terms of acuity and freedom from distortion. Such youngsters are spoken of as hard-of-hearing.

There is no simple way to determine which educational approach to take with hearing impaired children and to predict which children will achieve well in school or acquire the ability to use and understand oral language. As with all other children, there are some who are mentally gifted and some who mentally retarded. The circumstances of early life differ, too, for hearing impaired children. Some go undetected and understimulated. Others have sophisticated, intensive help from the first months of life. The nature of the hearing loss itself differs from child to child, though the net affect may seem to be the same in the sense that the child simply cannot hear. The actual degree and kind of hearing loss, as revealed by expert study, can be helpful in keeping it from growing worse and in deciding what kind of hearing aid, if any, should be prescribed. But relatively little can be predicted in detail about educational matters from study of the hearing loss.

In order to discover the most effective educational approach to hearing impaired children, special educators recommend the following:

1. Identify hearing impaired children as early in life as possible. For many, that can be done in the first few months of life.
2. Start as early as the child is identified to establish as many forms of communication as possible (oral, visual, tactual, kinesthetic).*
3. Follow systematic instructional procedures which call for perceptual and communication training throughout the child's waking hours every day of the week and every week of the year.

---

*Some special educators adhere to a solely oral procedure at this and ensuing levels, requiring the hearing handicapped child to rely entirely on speech reading (lipreading) and any residual hearing which might be employed with amplification.

(For examples of such procedures for the first three years of life, see Northcott, W. H., 1973.)

4. Move to specific instruction in the use of hearing aids; auditory training, the optimum use of what hearing remains; speech reading, what has in the past been called lipreading; and speech correction.

5. Give the child instruction in the same curriculum provided for nonhandicapped pupils at elementary, secondary and higher education levels. At the same time supply special education particularly for language development, including reading, speaking, writing, and comprehension of expressions whose meanings depend heavily upon the tone of the voice.

In the process of moving through those five steps, some hearing impaired children develop good quality oral speech and comprehension of others through speech reading and excellent reading and writing skills, and find a minimum of difficulty adapting socially and vocationally to the hearing world. Others do not, but learn to rely more and more on finger spelling, writing, and sign language for direct communication. That, of course, does not necessarily limit the extent of their education. It does tend to restrict the scope of adult social and vocational opportunities.

There is much speculation about why some hearing impaired pupils acquire an oral way of communication and others do not. It does not appear to be necessarily related to the degree or the nature of the early childhood hearing loss. It does not necessarily appear, either, to be closely related to the intelligence, teaching methods, or any other easily identified variable. One thing there is general agreement upon: the earlier in life systematic daily instruction can be initiated, the better is the chance that hearing impaired children will acquire high quality language, oral speech, and speech comprehension, the latter largely through visual means.

CHILDREN AND YOUTH WITH LEARNING DISABILITIES
Definition

Widely different meanings are attached to the term *learning disabilities*. Some are quite specific and others very general.

Originally the expression described particular learning problems, for example, weakness in the acquisition of orderly left-to-right eye progressions essential for reading, or the auditory misperceptions of sounds in words, or the visual misperceptions of printed letters (i.e. reversing *b* or *d*).

There is a very different meaning, however. It has a broader usage referring to many of the kinds of exceptional children mentioned earlier in this book. Thus, children with mental retardation, children who are deaf, and children with other handicaps which interfere with education may be grouped together as children with *learning disabilities*.

It is important to be aware of this dissonance in terminology. Unless educators and architects and others involved in a particular educational design enterprise use the term in the same way, costly misunderstandings can result.

We hope to bypass theoretical differences in orientation among educators in favor of stating positions on which there do seem to be agreements. These, then, can be used constructively by architects, educators, and others interested in structures and arrangements which facilitate learning on the part of handicapped pupils.

First, it is clearly possible to say that all children in need of special education, simply by virtue of that fact, have learning disabilities. Second, we have already referred to some groups of handicapped children whose educational problems have substantial similarity while being essentially different from those of other groups (i.e. visually impaired, hearing impaired, and mentally retarded children). They are not mutually exclusive groups. There are mentally retarded and hearing impaired children. Also, visually and hearing impaired pupils, as well as retarded pupils, can all have reading disabilities or can all be emotionally disturbed or both. Despite the overlaps, we have separated hearing and vision impaired, mentally retarded, and others for discussion in earlier sections.

Whom, then, do we present under the rubric of learning disabilities? We include children and youth to whom the following terms have been attached:

1. Children with the Strauss Syndrome.[150]
2. Emotionally disturbed children.
3. Brain injured and minimally brain damaged children.
4. Socially maladjusted children.

5. Children with specific special learning disabilities.
6. Hyperactive (hyperkinetic) children.
7. Perceptually handicapped children.
8. Developmentally imbalanced children.
9. Children with language disorders (dysfunctions).
10. Dyslexic children.
11. Children with maturational or developmental lags.

It is not our intent to impose a new way of organizing the terminology and group classifications of special education. Rather, we hope to limit our material to information highly relevant to designing schools and schooling for those handicapped children and youth. As we gathered information for that purpose, the organization for presenting the data emerged. Thus, in the truest sense, the organization (structure) of this book follows function as we view it.

Emotionally Disturbed Pupils

It is the affective or emotional aspect of education which needs special attention in certain children. Motor skills may be well developed. Reading, writing, and other cognitive achievements may be adequate. But self-control, socialization, or other similar behavior may represent the areas in which the child is an underachiever.

> Special education must somehow make the disturbed child's *occupation* as near like other children's *occupations* as can be tolerated.
> If disturbed children are to make a successful return to the regular classroom, they must be able to meet the academic and social requirements of regular classrooms.[130]

There are several controversial ideas regarding teaching emotionally disturbed children. These ideas are reflections on how the expression *emotionally disturbed* is defined and on the implications the educator draws from the definition. The ideas also cut across approaches to teaching all children with learning disabilities and can be grouped, as Bednar and Haviland[22] have, as follows:

DEVELOPMENTAL APPROACHES: These start with the notion that children progress through a sequence of phases and stages if their total growth is normal. They may be normally fast or slow (bright or dull), but correct development is steady, regular, even, and predictable. Broadly speaking, the main groupings of development are sensorimotor development, auditory and visual perception, language and cognitive development, and emotional and social development. Deficits in development can be noted in any or all groupings. Special education consists of applying measures to remedy the deficits.

PSYCHOTHERAPEUTIC APPROACHES: These are probably more medical than educational. The pupil is conceived of as having abnormal personality and social development. Reeducation is used as a psychotherapeutic treatment procedure under the direction of a psychiatrist or clinical psychologist. The child has the benefit of understanding, play therapy, counseling, and support for appropriate behavior. The teacher is guided by treatment directions.

BEHAVIOR MODIFICATION APPROACHES: These deal directly with the actual behavior of the pupil. Behavior which is maladaptive (i.e. not working at assigned task) is replaced by adaptive behavior (i.e. working at assigned task). The teacher manipulates pupil rewards and other environmental influences to bring the pupil to behave consistently in desired ways.

None of the above approaches have we found in schools in a *pure* state. However, it is usually possible to show that one or another is the dominant approach in use.

Other Educationally Retarded Pupils

MALADJUSTED CHILDREN: These children need learning opportunities capitalizing on their facility with the:
1. Physical and visual rather than the aural.
2. Content centered rather than form centered.
3. Externally oriented rather than introspective.
4. Problem centered rather than abstract centered.
5. Inductive rather than deductive.
6. Spatial rather than temporal.
7. Slow, careful, patient, persevering (in areas of importance) rather than quick, clever, facile, and flexible.[130]

CHILDREN WITH LANGUAGE DISORDERS (DYSFUNCTIONS): In the view of some educators, these children overlap with children having specific (special) learning disabilities, perceptual handicaps, and maturational or developmental lags.

In teaching a child with a *generalized deficiency in auditory learning,* the primary objective is to help him utilize all of his capacities.

1. If he cannot acquire spoken language, it is important for his protection that he learn to understand the meaning of the social sounds of his environment.
2. He should be able to sort out a particular sound from the conglomerate auditory world, know when to ignore it and when to respond.
3. He should, for example, be able to relate the sound of a train or a truck with the object and react appropriately.
4. Even if he can use sounds only for signalling or warning purposes, he will become more socially competent.
5. The ultimate goal, however, is to teach him to understand the meaning of both social sounds and the spoken word.
6. The primary task of the teacher is to help the child relate sounds to the proper units of experience, and in doing so, perhaps the fundamental instructional principle is simultaneity.[90]

A RECEPTIVE APHASIC: This youngster is one who has adequate hearing and intelligence but does not understand what is said to him in his native tongue. The primary educational goal for the receptive aphasic child is development of auditory language.[90] On the other hand, the primary objective in teaching the child with *deficits in oral expressive language* is the development of the auditory motor patterns for speaking. In this case, every effort is made to teach him control of oral musculature so that he can produce sounds and blend them into meaningful words.[90]

A VISUAL DYSLEXIC: This child or youth has not learned to read under ordinary methods of instruction despite evidence of capability to do so. *Reading disability* is also used to describe the condition. The purpose of the instruction is to give the pupil a systematic means of attacking words and to aid him in learning a sight vocabulary. The purpose of all reading instruction is to give the child a means of identifying the world he sees. The visual dyslexic frequently begins by learning the sounds of letters and integrating them into wholes. The *auditory dyslexic,* in contrast, works most frequently from the whole to the part in acquiring reading skill.[90]

DYSGRAPHIC CHILDREN: These children have unusual difficulty learning to write. Special education teachers begin by presenting visual and kinesthetic patterns separately, gradually working toward integration of the two.[90]

It must be apparent from the above material that the *learning disabilities* group is an aggregate of conditions which are not clearly linked together by common bonds of cause, of effect, or of management procedures for their amelioration and correction. Efforts are being made to improve the understanding of learning disabilities, and those efforts are leading the way toward more precise definition.

In 1962, Kirk and Bateman [99] said:

> A learning disability refers to a retardation, disorder, or delayed development in one or more of the processes of speech, language, reading, writing, arithmetic, or other school subjects resulting from a psychological handicap caused by a possible cerebral dysfunction and/or emotional or behavioral disturbances. It is not the result of mental retardation, sensory deprivation, or cultural or instructional factors.

In 1968, the National Advisory Committee on Handicapped Children [121] concluded that:

> A learning disability refers to one or more specific deficits in essential learning processes requiring special educational techniques for its remediation.
>
> Children with learning disabilities generally demonstrate a discrepancy between expected and actual achievement in one or more areas, such as spoken, read, or written language, mathematics and spatial orientation.
>
> The learning disability referred to is not primarily the result of sensory, motor, intellectual, or emotional handicap, or lack of opportunity to learn.
>
> Deficits are to be defined in terms of accepted diagnostic procedures in education and psychology.
>
> Essential learning processes are those currently referred to in behavioral science as perception, integration, and expression, either verbal or nonverbal.
>
> Special education techniques for remediation require educational planning based on the diagnostic procedures and findings.

In 1969, McCarthy and McCarthy [112] said, ". . . . we find few characteristics that are shared by all children identified as having learning disabilities." That statement seems to continue to hold. At the same time, however, estimates of the incidence and prevalence of learning disabilities continue to rise. A national projection that 3 percent of the school population is affected would be considered conservative.

Because of uncertainties connected both with definitions and incidence and prevalence figures, it is necessary to move with particular care in designing schools and schooling to accommodate the learning disabled population. Local projections based on specific survey data are highly advisable as a basis for planning.

CRIPPLED AND NEUROLOGICALLY IMPAIRED CHILDREN AND YOUTH

When stated in broad terms, the goals of education are essentially the same for handicapped as for nonhandicapped students. These goals may also need to be modified for a particular child on the basis of his physical condition and the extent to which it will continue to be a limiting factor in their attainment. However, education is aimed at assisting the pupil to achieve the fullest measure of self-realization of which he is capable and to become a contributing member of society to the limits of his capacity regardless of where he may be along the continuum of physical and mental capabilities.[98]

Definition

The crippled and neurologically impaired make up a heterogenous category. But before enumerating some of the diverse reasons why children would be so classified, it is important to remind ourselves of one of the limits of the definition of special education. There are (sadly) many handicapped children. But not all of them *need* special education. In fact, most do not. Our focus is only on those youngsters whose handicaps *interfere* with or *limit* the opportunity to acquire an education in the usual way. Thus, not all crippled, deformed, or health impaired children and youth are included; only those who require special education.

Today, the majority of children found in special classes and other programs for the physically impaired have problems of coordination, perception, and cognition (as well as mobility) resulting from the lack of proper development of, or injury to, the central nervous system. Today, the educator must be prepared not only to modify the classroom environment in terms of space, lighting, furniture, and equipment; but also to identify, evaluate, and remediate learning and adjustment problems peculiar to the neurologically impaired.[98]

Types

Many of the educational problems encountered in this classification are quite similar to those found among children with learning disabilities. Others have no learning disabilities as such. Instead, they have such complex physical involvements that they require a broad range of technical equipment such as special typewriters, page turners, standing tables, and other daily living assistance devices. It is often necessary to equip special rooms or buildings for their use.

Among the neurologically impaired, the largest single group is accounted for by cerebral palsy. In essence, cerebral palsy is abnormal body movement caused by damage to the brain. The same brain injury which results in motor disturbance can also result in learning difficulties, defects in hearing and vision, and convulsive disorders. It should come as no surprise, then, that speech problems and emotional problems might be present as well.

In public school programs for the physically handicapped, children with cerebral palsy account for one fourth to one third of the pupils. The rest are made up of youngsters with spina bifida, epilepsy, and a variety of orthopedic conditions and other health problems including muscular dystrophy, poliomyelitis, heart disease or defects, liver or kidney disorders, and respiratory disorders.

Incidence and Prevalence

It is really not possible to give educationally useful estimates of how many such children and youth can be expected to appear in a community. That is especially true since only *some* of the children with these conditions need special education, and that need must be determined individually. Therefore, it is necessary that each school district make and maintain its own inventory of physically handicapped and neurologically impaired pupils and keep a record of their special education needs. Planning can then be done on a more realistic basis.

School Settings

Historically, physically handicapped and neurologically impaired children and those with other severe continuing health problems were educated in hospitals, at home, or in special schools built for the purpose. The hospital school is described in Chapter I. Special schools are still common. However, they are taking on more and more the characteristics listed in Chapter I.

Home teaching is done by visiting teachers, telephonic communication, or both. In Los Angeles, a corp of teachers work from a central location to instruct groups of homebound pupils by intercommunicating telephones. In many cities and rural areas a single homebound child is linked to his regular class by an open telephone line. Signals allow the child to interrupt to ask questions or contribute to discussions. Where classes move from room to room or area to area, a *buddy* unplugs and moves the homebound child's receiver-speaker along with the class and plugs it in again.

It is advisable to tie in this possibility with the wiring of any new school. The location of the speaker-receiver can also be improved if it is *planned in* when schools are constructed.

The trend toward mainstreaming is seen plainly in the education of physically, neurologically, and health impaired pupils. The wide range of intellectual and creative ability among such children means that some of them may be integrated in honors classes, some in art studios, some in classes for the mentally retarded, some in vocational programs, and others in other components of the schools. That argues strongly that barrier-free regular schools must be the order of the day if equal educational opportunity is to be made available to these youngsters.

Procedures for Teaching

The teachers of physically, neurologically, and health impaired youngsters may well be among the most versatile of all members of the education professions. They must be skilled in applying instructional procedures ranging from those for gifted and talented pupils to those designed for children with specific learning disabilities. And they must be ready to apply the techniques in settings ranging from hospitals and special schools to the pupils' homes.

DEVELOPMENTAL DISABILITIES

A new term made its official entry into the special education lexicon with the passage of Public Law 91-517* by the Federal Congress. According to the law:

The term *developmental disability* means a disability attributable to

---

*Public Law 91-517, 91st Congress, S-2846, October 30, 1970.

mental retardation, cerebral palsy, epilepsy, or another neurological condition of an individual found by the Secretary to be closely related to
mental retardation or to require treatment similar to that required for
mentally retarded individuals, which disability originates before such
individual attains age eighteen, which has continued or can be expected
to continue indefinitely, and which constitutes a substantial handicap to
the individual.

Professional educators and psychologists find a number of problems
in translating that definition into operational language for special
education purposes. A particularly good discussion of the uncertainties and ambiguities, and an attempt to resolve them, is found in an
article by Neisworth and Smith.[125]

It is too early to be sure about what new impact, if any, will be
made on the special education of handicapped children and youth
by Public Law 91-517. One thing seems assured, however. The door
has been opened for more children to come legitimately under the
special education umbrella. Many youngsters are referred by teachers
to psychologists because the children are thought to be mentally retarded. Perhaps a fourth or a third are found by the psychologists
not to be mentally retarded as measured by intelligence quotient or
by social maturity. Yet the youngsters do react in school in ways
very similar to their mentally retarded classmates. Now, apparently,
the definition of *developmental disabilities* could make them eligible
for special education services. If so, two factors will emerge with
possible major affects on the space in which schooling is to be conducted.

First, there will be an increase in the proportion of school children
classified as in need of special education. That, in turn, will mean
that proportionately more of each school's space will need to be devoted to that purpose.

Second, a variety of new means of instruction will probably be
developed with attendant equipment and software. That, too, will
tend to call for more space of the kind which can be adapted to as
yet unforeseeable ways of teaching.

In short, the delineation of a new descriptive category for certain
kinds of handicapped pupils promises to call for increased special
education space and for a high level of flexibility in that space.

CHAPTER VI

GENERAL CONSIDERATIONS FOR HANDICAPPED PUPILS IN FACILITIES DESIGN

To THE BEST OF our judgment, the move toward open plan areas gives more opportunities for excellent education for handicapped pupils than more traditional school designs. However, each design group must weigh all of the pros and cons as they see them and come to their own decisions in the matter. An assessment of the values and limitations of the open plan arrangement may help in coming to a decision that will stand the test of the future.

The checklist which appears in this chapter is offered in the same spirit. It is clear that our viewpoint is one favoring inclusion. But we are sure that there could be situations where the weight would fall in the other direction.

OPEN PLAN SCHOOL CONCEPT*

In an open plan school several teachers and groups of pupils often share one large, open space in full view of each other. Noise levels and visual distraction prove less of a problem than might be thought. There is some acoustical spillage from one area to another, and the potential for problem noise is always present. However, the advantages of the open plan can outweigh such minor limitations. The walled in containment of conventional boxlike classrooms can reduce noise problems. However, such arrangements can also engender other serious limitations for team teaching.

The contemporary open plan has been the nation's fastest growing characteristic of new schools. More than 50 percent of all schools

*This section includes material from a report in the September, 1971 issue of *School House,* a newsletter for the Educational Facilities Laboratories, Inc., New York, N. Y.

built in the United States from September, 1968 to September, 1971 embody open plan design. Reports increase regarding how well modern educational approaches work under open space conditions.

High priority consideration must be given, in new or remodeled schools, to the open plan design. The design for open plan space can keep the best of the traditional and blend it with the modern. It can be flexible and transitional, often using movable partitions rather than fully open space. In keeping with current trends, that sort of plan would be dubbed *first generation open space.* Some areas are entirely open, while others, especially those requiring no special furnishings, are often divided by floor-to-ceiling partitions which are collapsible or demountable.

It can be hampering to attempt to operate modern educational programs in a school building of traditional design. Success is much more likely for more advanced concepts of educational programming in an open facility.

Teachers and pupils adapt readily to the open space. In addition to allowing more freedom to use a variety of modern teaching procedures, the open space situation fosters the development of consideration and good manners on the part of all concerned.

Open space furnishings are commonly chairs, stools, or hassocks which are movable enough to accommodate up to six students at a table. The carpeted floors allow pupils to use pillows to sit or to stretch directly on the floor for variation in study conditions.

To create a *sense of territory* for groups or individuals, portions of the open space can be delineated by using visual displays, movable chalkboards, and alterations in lighting level and types of lighting. Visual overload and distraction need to be avoided and that is best accomplished by limiting the array of colors and shapes in the open space.

Open plan schools adapt well to the varying life styles of pupils and to varying teaching styles. Such schools make it possible to open the curriculum, to open the school, to experiment, and to change. They are regarded by most of those who have tested them as far superior to traditional schools for providing high quality education for today's children.

As teaching experience in the free, flexible space plan schools increases, we may expect that the practice will extend to instruction for the handicapped. In reality, open space on a small scale has been the pattern of instruction for handicapped children for many years. Even most regular classrooms could never again attain the structured regimentation of orderly rows of desks which was once thought to be the best of all arrangements for instruction.

A PLACE IN WHICH TO TEACH

For many years we interpreted the need for visual and auditory privacy in learning areas as requiring these areas to be enclosed by floor to ceiling walls and entered by a closable doorway. Today, experience with open space in regular schools for normal children has clearly demonstrated that the rigidity of enclosing walls is not essential to effective learning, nor may it be most desirable. Many of the open learning areas have shown that visual barriers, where needed, may be as simple as movable furniture, chalkboards, or tack-boards at eye level.

Auditory barriers are not created quite so simply. A sound-absorbing carpeted floor is necessary, and a ceiling of acoustic tile is essential as the minimum of control. To a certain extent, sound itself is its own barrier, given different learning groups occupying a single space. If the groups are separated by a few feet and each group is generating approximately the same volume of noise, they do not interfere with each other. On the other hand, if the intensity of sound between the two groups is significantly different, learning areas will not be compatible. A rhythm band practicing near the same space where a group of children are doing written exercises in arithmetic would definitely interfere with the latter.

The problem of planning learning space is made less difficult if we analyze the characteristics of the group instruction that the space is expected to serve. If it is typical of the usual discussions or instruction at normal voice levels, one group will not interfere with another. The same can be said for the small groups or even the individual instruction that is a major portion of the teaching of handicapped children.

Ideally, the instructional area for handicapped children will have spatial variety: high space, low space, small space, and large space.

There should be a place for a single child to work or lounge independently, and a space for companions to work together. Some instruction will best be given to small groups, and other instructions may be given to a large group, all of it equally effective. Some of these may be graded groups and some may not. Some space should be isolated to serve noisy activities. Other space may be isolated in order to serve experiences that are wet and messy and require more than average control of dampness, paint, clay, or sand.

Frequently, child accessible storage space is called for which has the potential for the pupil to follow a sequential storage and retrieval pattern of duplicated exercises on his own or with only visual supervision from an adult. In some instances, the pupils work with recorders, transcribers, projection apparatus, enlarged type books, tangible maps, globes and diagrams, and other bulky materials.

In summary, there should be a variety of learning spaces to suit the teacher's teaching objectives.

Spatial variety will overcome the monotony and possible boredom of inflexible walled enclosures. Further stimulus can be added by a variety of light sources with rheostatic control of light in certain areas. Light can change the visual character of instructional space from a totally brightly lit display area to the other extreme, a dimly lit area with concentrated light focusing on a single center interest much like a theater-in-the-round.

The flexible enclosure of space, freedom to change the distribution of furniture, and variety in the location of visual barriers and controlled lighting can give the teacher the options necessary to lead children to a stimulating variety of experiences. Combine these characteristics with a color scheme that gives delight, with a variety in the tactile qualities of all of the things the child touches, with an exciting scheme of graphics on walls or even on ceilings, and the result will be instructional space physically enriched to its maximum.

TRAFFIC PATTERNS

When everyone is locked into patterns of control and held there for months or years, school experience becomes damagingly narrowed. "Sit here, no talking, go straight down hall B to the next class, go home at 3:15, don't look in the wrong stacks . . ."

Organization managers are learning that all this has to be reversed: that random patterns must be encouraged, the mix of groups changed often, oldsters put with youngsters, the walls moved, the vista changed. Open space schools have discovered that visible traffic becomes quite innocuous to learning activities if it is part of the natural life of the school. With the elimination of corridors, traffic motion through much of the school space can be direct, almost as the crow flies, without creating distraction. In some circumstances where it may be disruptive, visual screens can be used to block it off.

STORAGE

Too much storage of things reflects a dryness of process. When not much is expected to happen, things are put away in anticipation of possible later use. Eventually they become abandoned. Storage, in fact, turns out to be one of the most static and expensive things we do, given the cost of the raw square footage it consumes, plus case work, combined with lost or forgotten equipment. The answer is a lightfooted, versatile service system that provides fewer closed cabinets and drawers and more open shelving, preferably on wheels for easy movement to dispensing points.

ELASTICITY OF SPACE

Nonetheless, a concept of perfectly filled space does remain important because it deals with a basic human inclination. People in a space always seek the right fit. We are all familiar with the tension felt in an overcrowded room or the eeriness of being alone in a gymnasium. Such maladjustments cause persistent discomfort. In turn, this intrudes into the work at hand by draining energy into an unresolvable search for *the right feeling*.

Properly viewed, an open facility is a space that breathes. Its elastic properties allow choice and variety, including enclosure to the degree desired. Moreover, the more critical aspects of territoriality have to do with communication privacy that is both visual and auditory.

SOUND

There are situations, however, in which some kinds of sound suppression are useful. When an environment is full of hard surfaces, as in the case of most schools, it is prone to be clangorous and reverberant. This can distort the sound of normal activities like walking or closing a door to a point where it interferes with oral communication and becomes an irritating intrusion into our conscious awareness. Carpeting, of course, has become the major tool for solving this problem.

An early example of carpeting as a sound suppressant is found in a school building owned by the Special School District of St. Louis County, Missouri. It has classes for mentally retarded pupils who also have learning disabilities which are often related to distractibility or the Strauss Syndrome.[149] According to the school official in charge, Assistant Superintendent Dr. John Kidd, the carpeting has proven effective, durable, and attractive.

The sounds of a music or shop area, for example, are not likely to be compatible with a foreign language teaching area. Planning and scheduling of appropriate adjacencies are necessary.

THE LEARNING CENTER

To stimulate children's interest, some schools have added a learning center, recognizing that arousing a child's interest is a precondition leading to a success experience. The corollary is also true. Success experiences intensify interest and encourage further effort.

The learning center can combine colored lights, stained glass, a mural painting wall, a story pit, a wet space for clay and water play and finger painting, a scrap bin, a *dress up* corner with costume clothes, a green house, animal cages, an aquarium, an adding machine, a typewriter, a calculator, and a tape recorder. The list of inexpensive, practical and durable articles that will interest and stimulate children is almost endless. The imagination of the teacher can provide an assortment that will provoke an excited response that can be as stimulating for the handicapped as for normal children—and much more necessary to those whose experiences have been limited.

CLASS SIZE

Special education classes have traditionally been substantially smaller than others. The range may extend from about five pupils (young deaf pupils or very difficult emotionally disturbed pupils) to as many as twenty-five pupils (homogeneously grouped educable mentally retarded pupils of high school age). Even the highest of those figures is markedly below, for example, the thirty-six to thirty-seven average regular class size revealed by a 1972 survey in Cleveland.

The major reason for smaller class sizes in special education is the need for the teacher to apply sharply increased individualization of instruction. The special education teacher often has to create very personalized lesson plans, to locate or make instructional materials to help implement the lesson plans, and to do all this in the context of a group of pupils with limitations of mobility, communication, attention span, sensory perception, or with other impediments to teaching.

Class size is usually specified for various kinds and levels of special education by the state education agency. Since there are differences from state to state, it is preferable to refer to the state regulations or, as they are sometimes called, the standards for the organization and administration of special education. These can be obtained without charge from the office of the state director of special education. For purposes of illustration, the following material on class size has been drawn from "Program Standards for Special Education," Ohio Department of Education, Columbus, June 30, 1973.

HANDICAPPING CONDITION	*.CLASS SIZE*
Hearing Impaired (Deaf and Hard-of-Hearing)	6 to 8
Crippled (Orthopedically and Other Health Impaired)	8 to 16
Visually Impaired (Blind and Partially Seeing)	8 to 12
Severe or Multiple Impairments (Deaf/Blind, Autistic, Aphasic)	Unspecified
Learning and Behavioral Disabilities (Neurologically Handicapped and Emotionally Handicapped)	8 to 10
Severe Behavioral Handicaps (Emotionally Disturbed)	6 to 15
Educable Mentally Retarded:	
Elementary or Junior High School	12 to 18
Senior High School	14 to 22
Speech, Language, and Hearing Services (Speech Disorders, Comprehensive and Expressive Language Disturbances, Voice Disorders, Stuttering, and Hearing Deficits)	Case Load of 60 to 110

Children with mental retardation below the educable range are served by Department of Health and Welfare programs in Ohio. In other states they tend to be included in public school provisions, with class size ranging from eight to fifteen, depending on the ages of the pupils and their capabilities.

Class size figures such as the above are applicable for pupil accounting purposes whether the classes are separate entities or whether the special education pupils are with other children in mainstream or in some other degree of integration with regular classes.

No one has adequately determined the size of a class for most effective learning. In some states, as we have seen, and in some countries, the number of children under the direction of a single teacher is established by law. But the size of a group that promotes maximum learning is still a variable which must be gauged by the teacher in the local setting. Some children will learn some things better alone. Certain children will learn better when within arm's reach of their teacher. Some will learn more from the other children than from their teacher. Others must be part of a group, whether large or small, and need the reinforcement of their peers. Whatever the children's need may be, space should be available to the teacher to vary the learning setting to suit the teaching objective and to make the learning experience most profitable. We emphasize again that teachers of handicapped children must have options. The physical space must not get in the way but should intensify and enrich the experience.

SPACE PER PUPIL

It is expected that improved architectural solutions to a number of major space utilization problems will be created each time a new school is planned. Therefore, it can be anticipated that certain areas will decrease square footage demand because more efficient and more effective architectural interpretations will be devised.

At the same time it can be predicted that each passing year will produce more technical equipment and instructional material aimed at helping teachers improve their productivity. Such apparatus and printed material tend to enlarge the space requirements per pupil, especially in the early years of use before standardization and miniaturization can be accomplished. Also, every year certain pressures bring new and important educational tasks to the schools as more and more additions are made to the curriculum, and fewer and fewer items are allowed to be dropped from the work expected from the schools. Thus, the educator and the architect are hard put to maintain a balance, and space requirements per pupil tend to increase.

Targets which seem reasonable for space per pupil in newly constructed or remodeled elementary, middle, and high schools are given below.

Classification	*Grades*	*Enrollment**	*Square Feet Per Pupil*
Elementary	K to 5	1,000	95
Middle	6 to 8	1,600	130
High	9 to 12	2,700	140

If the above per pupil square footage figures were graphed, it would be seen that there is almost a straight-line progression in the increase of total space per pupil from elementary through high school. One obvious reason for the upward trend is in the actual size of the pupils. Tenth grade youths are almost twice as large as third grade pupils. While they do not need twice the space, it is reasonable that they would need more. Another reason more space is needed in higher grades is the steady increase in the complexity of pupil programs. The incremental expansion of subject matter and related activities from mathematics and band and chemistry to typing and studio art and athletics is paralleled by an accumulation of equipment, apparatus, books, and other instructional materials, all of which must be conveniently and safely accommodated in the school. These two factors appear to accelerate at a steady and similar rate over the school years, from elementary through middle school to high school, and together they account for much of the increase in required space per pupil.

Generally, the younger the child, the greater the tendency to self contained instructional space. As the child moves from preschool to primary and intermediate levels of learning and experiences an increasing need for self-expression and self-generated activities, the instructional space must be modified to provide greater flexibility and increasingly promote social interaction.

Learning space for children with certain handicaps must be modi-

---

*The enrollment column is included for a reference baseline only. It can be expected that square footage per pupil will need to increase in smaller schools.

fied by reason of the handicap. The visually disabled will require space for bulky equipment in addition to learning space that emphasizes tactile experiences. There will be record players, recorders, braille books, braille writers, typewriters, talking book machines and magnifying reading machines. Braille books will require shelving that allows unusually large books (fifteen-by-fifteen-inch) to stand on edge.

Instructional space for hearing-impaired children will also have special characteristics. Since schooling for deaf children frequently begins at age three or earlier, provision must be made for the toileting, dressing, and general care of young children. The learning space must also be designed to eliminate all extraneous noise and reduce reverberation to a minimum. Some learning areas have been designed with the rear wall as a sounding board to reinforce and focus the voice of the teacher. When children have no hearing whatsoever, classrooms have been designed with wood floors on sleepers to allow the teacher to signal to the group through vibration of the floor. A tap of the foot will secure their attention.

In view of today's problem of increasing burglary and theft, and considering the many valuable portable pieces of instructional equipment, provision should be made for adequate lockable storage rooms. Many pieces are too heavy to carry and will be moved on wheeled carts. The storage area must be large enough to accommodate all of the carts since this equipment will normally be in the learning areas during the school day. The storage room may be used for other purposes during school hours.

GUIDELINES FOR SPACE NEEDED

Small [147] finds current guidelines for educational space, particularly for young children, too vague. She quotes Gardner [73] to illustrate. "The physical environment should be comfortable, spacious, and stimulating, enhancing the relationships among children, teachers, parents, administrators, and the community."

Small goes on to criticize such characteristic statements by saying:

"To define a physicosocial environment by stating that it should be "comfortable, spacious, and stimulating" is to give an unusable recipe. These recipes for learning environments are like recipes for a cake which state: "The cake should be tasty and moist; the appropriate amount of each ingredient will make it so!" Even with a cake, a relatively simple product which appeals mainly to the gustatory sense, it is necessary to know how much of what to use, in what order, and quite importantly, too, the preference of the potential eater."

In order to have usable guidelines, the design team needs as much detailed information as possible from the special educator about how space will be used and what it needs to be able to contain at its maximum usage peak.

RELATION OF SPACE TO SOCIAL BEHAVIOR MODIFICATION

The education of handicapped children cannot be divorced from problems of behavior modification since most of the children will engage in abnormal and undesirable behavior to some degree. The social behavior of some will be quite adequate, but others will produce inadequate social behavior in an attempt to reduce their tensions. Not all children will relieve their tensions in the same way.

Mild emotional stress may be dealt with by a short period of isolation in a *time-out* room, a small enclosed space contiguous with the learning area, which allows the teacher to observe the child through unbreakable glass. The child may seek out the *time-out* room voluntarily or be isolated as a disciplinary measure.

The more severe emotional stress of some handicapped children may cause sudden and uncontrollable noise, extremely destructive aggressive action, repetitive acts, or completely unpredictable explosions. The problem is not mainly the provision of a *time-out* room or even a *bang-room* where the upset pupil can hammer out his fury, but, rather, concern for the protection of the child so he does not harm himself or others. An isolation room away from the learning area will best serve the purpose, provided that it is under supervision. Normally, each school will have an isolation or holding room for children who become sick and must wait the arrival of a parent. This can serve a multiple purpose if furnished sparsely with indestructible items, including unbreakable glass in light fixtures and observation windows.

Problems of behavior will diminish for some children if they are relieved from long periods of sitting on hard seats or in close proximity to other pupils. Until recently, formal academic learning took place with the class seated in a regular pattern at typical desks, and overlooked the fact that teaching might be more effective if the children were more comfortable. A wider variety of permissible postures will automatically relieve tension.

Physiological research tells us that sitters tend not to live as long as those who live and work with more postural variation. It is ironic that the first thing we teach a child is to sit quietly for long periods on a hard seat. The question is, what are the postural patterns that are compatible with teaching and learning activities?

The sensible objective is to allow wide postural variation. Open space schools, with their space and seating manipulatory ability, their carpeted floors, have the option for more variety. It is entirely plausible to conduct discussions with students in standing, leaning, or perching postures. Reading is more naturally accommodated in lounging or even floor postures.

Given a free choice, a child will seek a space that comfortably accommodates the work to be done, and the child will fit into that space. The chosen posture may be standing, leaning, lounging with feet higher than head, perching on a stool or rail, or lying on the floor on back or stomach. Some schools have tried small boxlike enclosures with vision holes and a larger opening to crawl into. Others use rugs and heaps of pillows. All are innovations providing spatial variety, furniture variety, and a high degree of postural variety to relieve tensions and accordingly improve behavior and academic performance.

SCHOOLS SERVING HANDICAPPED PUPILS

Schools serving exceptional children can be classified as follows:

Regular Schools

Nursery-Kindergarten
Elementary Schools
Middle Schools
Junior High Schools
Senior High Schools
Vocational/Technical Schools
Two-Year College

Four-Year College
Universities

Special Schools

Hospital Schools
Day Schools
Residential Schools
Home Schools

It may be surprising at first, but all kinds of exceptional children and youth can be found receiving high quality special education in all of those settings. Historically, as was noted earlier, certain handicapped children were associated with certain schools. Examples are crippled children with special day schools and deaf or blind children with residential schools.

Rapid and recent technological changes in education plus a social demand for integration of all kinds are major factors which have brought handicapped and nonhandicapped pupils together in the same school situations. That trend is growing. One result has been a turnaround in school planning and design away from the direction of special schools or suites or wings for handicapped pupils toward inclusion of facilities for handicapped pupils in all schools.

That does not mean that there are to be *no* special schools or wings or suites or self-contained centers. Rather, it means such units could diminish in number and would be used only for those youngsters who are clearly unable, for the time being, to join with nonhandicapped pupils in regular schools. And it is expected that such youngsters could be much fewer than was once thought.

It seems clear that two major messages for architects are found in that new trend. One is that all regular school buildings may be planned and designed to contain the adjustments for handicapped children and youth once reserved for special schools. The second is that those special schools, wings, or suites which are constructed in the future may need to have two characteristics they have not had in the past. They will primarily need to be able to accommodate children with more severe and complex handicaps than before. Also, they will need to be readily remodeled or otherwise adapted to become effective schools for nonhandicapped persons. Otherwise, they may have to be abandoned as the swift moving current of educational technology advances to the point where the more severely handicapped, too, are integrated into regular schools.

LOCATION OF PLANT AND FACILITIES

We have seen excellent special education programs being conducted in the same buildings and instructional space as regular education for all other children. We have also seen excellent special education programs being conducted in buildings and rooms entirely separate from those of all other children.

As a general rule, special education should be brought into the regular class for the pupils who need it rather than have pupils removed from the regular class and taken to special classes or schools. We know this can be done successfully and economically in most instances for all varieties of exceptional children. We are also aware that not all exceptional children can best be accommodated full-time, or sometimes not even part-time, in regular classes, no matter how much support is supplied to the regular teacher. Thus, how special education service is delivered is not an *either/or* matter. It calls for a continuum of possibilities to be fitted to the individual case.

Neither complete integration nor complete segregation is the *right* or *wrong* pattern for all children. The issue needs continuing study, and we are aware that different communities, in the meantime, will take one or another point of view on the matter, depending upon local conditions. We may be certain that all will aim toward high quality special education for all exceptional children. That can be accomplished within a variety of organizational and administrative patterns.

The kinds of information needed to develop the most productive interface between the teaching environment and the teacher-learner interaction follow in a CHECK LIST which can be used to help make determinations about the setting in which special education is to be located.

School administrators and boards of education often seek help in making decisions about the location and design of physical plant and facilities to be used in the education of exceptional children. This check list, located in Figure 1., a, b, and c, is designed to give assistance in that situation.

CHECK LIST OF CONSIDERATIONS IN THE LOCATION OF SPECIAL EDUCATION PHYSICAL PLANT AND FACILITIES*

TERMS USED TO CLASSIFY EXCEPTIONAL CHILDREN

Blind
Partially Seeing
Deaf
Hard-of-Hearing
Mentally Retarded
   a. Trainable
   b. Educable
Learning Disabilities
Perceptual Disorders
Minimal Brain Damage

Neurologically Impaired
Behavior Disorder
Speech Handicapped
Socially Maladjusted
Crippled
Chronic Health Problems
Emotionally Disturbed
Gifted
Multiply Exceptional

EDUCATIONAL FACILITIES

1. Regular classroom with consultant to teacher.
2. Resource room and regular classroom combination.
3. Special classes in regular schools.
4. Wings on regular schools.
5. Separate special day schools.
6. Separate special residential schools.

Factors for Consideration	Exceptional Children	Location of Educational Facilities					
		1	2	3	4	5	6
1. Does the location facilitate scheduled participation in regular classes and transfer to and from regular classes when the educational needs of the exceptional child can best be met by such arrangements?							
2. Does the location provide maximum opportunities for exceptional children to test reality; to have lifelike problems to meet and to overcome?							
3. Is the location one which provides the most flexibility in the use of school plant?							
4. Are there enough pupils to provide for suitable groupings by age, ability, and achievement?							
5. Are the needed kinds of specialized staff available?							
6. Is participation with normal children in the following school activities facilitated by the location?							
a. Sports and physical education, including corrective							
b. Music, including vocal groups, orchestra, and band							

*This check list was developed by Dr. Jack W. Birch.

Factors for Consideration	Exceptional Children	Location of Educational Facilities					
		1	2	3	4	5	6
c. Forensics and plays							
d. Newspaper and yearbook							
e. Spectator sports and special events							
f. Class officers and student government							
g. Social events							
h. Auditorium programs							
i. Home economics							
j. Business education programs							
7. Is maximum use made of:							
a. School library							
b. School cafeteria							
c. Auditorium							
d. Shops							
e. Home economics suite							
f. Health services suite							
g. Gymnasium							
h. Swimming pool							
i. Outdoor recreation area							
8. Is the necessary specialized equipment available?							
9. Does the location facilitate transportation?							
10. Are audio-visual aids, maps, globes, language labs, and other expensive instructional materials made available to maximum extent by the location?							
11. Does the location foster the most efficient use of specialized personnel who can serve across the range of normal children and exceptional children?							
a. Principals							
b. Guidance counselors							
c. Speech therapists							
d. Psychologists							
e. School social workers							
f. Physicians							
g. Nurses							
h. Attendance officers							
12. Does the location maximize the use of supervisors in the skills and special fields and the subject areas?							

Factors for Consideration	Exceptional Children	Location of Educational Facilities					
		1	2	3	4	5	6
13. Does the location foster professional growth and fellowship among the special education teacher and all other teachers?							
14. Does the location foster professional growth and fellowship among the special education teachers?							
15. Does the location foster teamwork among special and regular teachers?							
16. Does the location increase the likelihood that brothers and sisters of exceptional children will attend school with them?							
17. Does the location increase the likelihood that children from the same neighborhoods will attend school together?							
18. Will the location enhance participation by parents of exceptional pupils in PTA, PTSA, and other parent groups?							
19. Will the location increase the chances that all children can make use of academic and social enrichment activities?							
20. Does the location have advantages in keeping the unit cost of building to a minimum?							
21. Does the location maximize the possibility of developing favorable community attitudes and understanding toward the work of the schools?							

ADDITIONAL NOTES:

1. If a special facility or special classes are to be included in or attached to a regular school, it is important that the regular school population be large enough initially to readily tolerate the degree of fusing or integration of students that may be anticipated without overwhelming the regular class teachers.

2. When an integrated program is planned, it will depend very greatly for its success on the readiness of the principal and regular teachers to foster it.

The check list grew from consulting experiences in a number of states and in different kinds of communities. The list probably does not include all the factors which will influence decisions. Some of the items are more relevant than others, and certain factors may be weighed differently in different situations. All of the items are considered to be of educational significance.

On the left at the top of the check list are terms used to describe children in need of special education. To use the check list for a certain group of exceptional children, put the name of the group in the column under the heading "Exceptional Children," and answer the questions under "Factors for Consideration."

At the top of the same page on the right are listed six different approaches to establishing educational facilities for the exceptional, from regular school facilities to separate schools. Some approaches are considered more desirable than others. It is generally accepted that exceptional children have the right to a sound education suited to their needs. It is also agreed that their education should be provided as near as possible under normal circumstances and in regular schools with other children. To use this part of the check list, indicate in the column headed "Location of Educational Facilities," to the right of the questions, the number of the setting which combines desirability and feasibility.

Some exceptional children have problems which make it necessary or advisable that they be educated in separate schools. They tend to be among a small minority of the exceptional. An important objective with these children is to foster their development, if possible, to the point at which they can be transferred to more desirable placements.

MOVEMENT TOWARD MAINSTREAMING

The automobile age, beginning in the early decades of this century, triggered improved ways to deliver children to more comprehensive and more modern schools. Along with all the rest of the children came those who were crippled and those who had other handicaps. First, handicapped pupils were assembled in special schools designed just for them. That was the era of the *special schools*.

Now handicapped pupils attend regular schools more often. They have even more advanced technical improvements in buses, lifts, motorized wheel chairs, and advances in architecture which minimize steps and other barriers to mobility. Improved surface transportation first brought handicapped children out of their homes and into centralized schools in which a real improvement in their educational opportunities was offered. Now there is a move, supported by more flexible surface transportation, to deliver even severely handicapped pupils to regular schools which have been designed or remodeled to accommodate their mobility, safety, and other requirements.

The move toward educating handicapped pupils in regular grades accelerated in the early 1970s because of social action pressures. As a result, mainstreaming emerged as a key concept. Under that concept, many handicapped pupils are the responsibility of regular class teachers with support and consultation from special educators. Other special education arrangements are used, of course, for the pupils who cannot yet be adequately educated in regular classes. But the mainstreaming approach meets the needs of 70 to 80 percent of exceptional children in some school districts.[30]

CHANGES IN RESIDENTIAL AND DAY SCHOOLS

Before 1940, special education tended to be decidedly isolated from regular education. As was mentioned earlier, America and other nations are dotted with special residential schools and special day schools mostly built between the 1880s and the 1930s.

The special residential and special day schools experienced marked changes in functions during the decades of the 1950s and 1960s, and the changes are still in progress. The most significant changes are these:

1. More children with multiple, complex educational problems are being accepted.
2. Initial intake students have tended to drop in age from about six years to two, to three years, and in some cases to infancy.
3. Many special residential and day schools have become short-term facilities for students needing intensive work, perhaps combined with paraeducational help in medical fields.
4. There has been increased interest in developing smaller residential schools, halfway houses, and day centers in or near

major population areas, with more emphasis on integrating handicapped persons into the larger community.

A fine example of a short-term day school linked to a regular elementary school is the Holladay Center for Handicapped Children operated by the Portland (Oregon) Public Schools. Their public information statement about the school says:

> The classrooms at Holladay Center are ungraded and self-contained. They are divided into preschool, primary, intermediate, and upper levels. To provide for special instructional and physical needs, each class is staffed by a teacher and an aide. Depending upon enrollment, more than one classroom may be designated for the same level. Age, skill development, severity of handicap, and personal development are criteria for movement from one class to another. The highest level students are assigned to the team room with two teachers and two aides. Teachers of music and art supplement the program in each classroom.
>
> The educational objectives and curriculum parallel those of regular elementary classrooms, even though special education methodologies are employed. A multidisciplinary approach affords classroom reinforcement of therapeutic efforts in such areas as language and speech development, initial writing and typing skills, and self-help skills. Also, the therapists largely determine and often design or make the adaptive equipment used in the classroom (electric typewriter and keyboard guards, typing mitts, pencil holders, head and mouth stylus, enlarged manipulative materials, cutout tables).
>
> When a child has reached a satisfactory level of development in all areas, he will be considered for integration into a regular classroom. Integration usually begins with partial integration into our adjoining elementary school before full-time integration into a neighborhood school.
>
> If a child continues to profit from our educational and therapeutic program until age sixteen, he may continue his learning in a setting commensurate with his abilities.

These changes in direction have brought with them new design and program problems as well as the need for a substantial remodeling of both structure and program in older facilities.

| CHAPTER VII |

SPECIFIC CONSIDERATIONS FOR
HANDICAPPED PUPILS IN FACILITY DESIGN

THE SECTIONS OF this chapter are organized under such topics as safety, movement, and self-care rather than by age groups or categories of handicaps. The topical arrangement chosen seems the most functional for persons interested in the design and construction of school facilities. First, these specific topics are important for all handicapped pupils. Second, many specific items apply to children in several handicapped groups, and when put together in this way, much repetition is avoided. Third, provisions which are essential for some children are sometimes also desirable for others. This arrangement makes it easy to show that. And fourth, thoughtful and broad scale planning can have the result that *all* schools are designed to be readily adaptable for habitation by all varieties of exceptional children and youth, as well as by professional and support staff members who may themselves be handicapped.

MOVEMENT

The deficit in the educational progress of many handicapped children is materially affected by their inability to move normally. Their educational experiences are reduced accordingly. They have not done all of the things that normal children do; consequently, their physical school environment must minimize this disability, make movement easy and safe, maximize the opportunities for new experiences, and thus create a rich stimulus for their curiosity and their desire to learn.

Movement must be viewed broadly to include the child's own bodily movements, the changing of the child's position by mechanical means, and movement in the environment. The child should be free to learn and free of concerns for the limitations of movement, because the physical environment has foreseen the problems and overcome them in so far as this may be possible.

Helps are sometimes essential but hopefully inconspicuous. They should not be so excessively *helpful* as to not encourage the development of self-sufficiency and self-confidence.

The child cannot concentrate on the learning task without the knowledge and confidence that the physical environment is safe. It must foresee falling, bumping, tripping, and slipping. It must foresee escape from a hazardous panic situation. Above all, the handicapped child must feel safe and secure and ready to learn.

Patterns of movement or required routes should be simple, not confusing, easily grasped, not frightening or surprising. If change is required, it should be anticipated. A confused, frightened child cannot learn.

Mainstream Arrangements

A school may serve both normal and handicapped children, or it may be designed for only the handicapped. In either case, the problems of mobility must be analyzed to insure that the children may move with ease and assurance around and through the school. Some will be able to walk and run. Others may be confined to wheelchairs or litters. Some will be on crutches. Whatever their physical, mental, or emotional state may be, thoughtful planning will recognize that the child's acceptance of the learning environment will reflect his assurance that it has not created problems with which he is unable to cope. Traffic patterns should be obvious. Obstacles must be clearly marked. Vision should be unobstructed, while the scale and character of the space should be warm and friendly. Strange buildings can be confusing and frightening for the child who is out of his home for the first time.

Arriving and Departing

Children who are handicapped may arrive and depart on foot, in taxis, by school bus, or with a parent in the family car. Regardless of how they arrive the tendency is still to have them come at approximately the same time. They will be of all ages. Some will be less mobile than others. All will require careful supervision. Many will require help. The degree of inevitable confusion and hazard will depend on the thoughtfulness of the designer. Even in a large school, both can be held to a minimum by planning carefully.

If the school enrolls both normal and handicapped children, it is desirable to provide a separate entrance for possible use by the handicapped. They may not all choose to use it, but for those who cannot take the buffeting of normal children, it will be there. In any case, all entrances should be without architectural barriers.

Regardless of the size of the school, a separate entrance should be provided for the nursery-kindergarten and other preschool age handicapped children. These smaller children will require more control. Many will be brought by a parent who must park and leave the car to deliver and pick up one or more children. The procedure will be simplified if a separate traffic lane is provided to serve the very early childhood units and the nursery-kindergarten, and if their fenced-in playground is immediately adjacent to the loading-unloading area. This will allow a minimum number of adults to safely control a maximum number of children. For departures, it allows the children to put on their outdoor clothing and play within sight of the arriving parent, taxi, or bus.

Factors of Climate

Where winter climate brings rain and snow, protection of the children should be provided at the arrival-departure area because of the time required by many to transfer from a vehicle to a wheelchair. The area should be roofed for protection from rain, and, if located in cold climates, the walks should be heated to remove snow and ice. Heat lamps are often installed to warm the children and aides. The site plan may permit this covered area to serve also as a covered play area during the school day, provided the adjacent traffic is controlled. Where climate is extreme, some schools have provided a large, enclosed, heated loading room with automatic overhead doors. Buses, taxis, and cars drive directly through a portion of the building. Opposite adjustments, similar in principle, may be advantageous in extremes of heat and dust storms. The degree of the exposure and the health of the children will determine the most effective economical scheme of protection.

Styles of Doors

From the arrival-departure area the children should be protected until they reach the doors to the school. If these are hand operated, wide single doors are preferable to the usual 5'-0" wide double doors. The latter requires that both doors be open for the convenient access of adult sized wheelchairs. If the budget is sufficiently generous, some automatic doors are desirable for they give pupils opportunities to practice using them. These will normally meet the requirements of building codes, but since they can swing only outward, there is an element of hazard if they strike a child when operating. A preferable, safer solution to the problem of entrance doors is an automatic sliding door, something children should also learn to manipulate. This is not considered an acceptable legal exit in the event of fire and panic, so when a sliding door is used, the building code will normally require adjacent swinging doors as well. Since many of the children are physically smaller than normal and may be less strong, ball bearing door hardware should be selected that will permit six- and seven-year-olds to operate the doors if they are not automatic. This would apply equally to doors throughout the building and particularly to the heavier metal clad doors required for fire separation or protection.

Wheelchair Parking

When wheelchairs, litters, or wagons remain at the school, an ample parking area will be required immediately adjoining the arrival-departure area to hold the vehicles until the child returns. This may be a lockable separate room, but if security is not a problem, it will be more convenient as a large alcove beside the vestibule or entrance corridor. It may even be an extension of the vestibule. If there is more than one arrival-departure area, each will require vehicle parking space.

Getting the School Day Under Way

The first activity on arrival will be the removal of coats, hats, and sometimes boots. Following this, many of the children require immediate toileting, particularly if they have been in a bus or taxi any length of time. If the school is not large, the coat room and toilet rooms may be adjacent to the entrance with supplementary toilets in the teaching area. However, the confusion of large numbers of children at the entrance in larger schools may be reduced by providing coat hanging space either near or within the teaching areas and toilets convenient to both the entrance and the teaching area. The corridor space in the arrival-departure area should be generous to facilitate arrival and also to provide a holding area at departure time when children are waiting for transportation. As already mentioned for nursery-kindergarten, a controlled playground can also serve as the holding area for larger children. Fences and low walls will help to contain them and keep them away from hazardous areas. Hedges may help but lack positive control.

The ease with which a child moves from the point of arrival to the teaching-learning area will contribute to his readiness to begin a learning task. His environment must be clearly defined and constant. Too much flexibility in choice and decision may be confusing. Changing finishes of walls and floors can give a directional sense. Easily identifiable landmarks will help. Changes in ceiling height will encourage movement. Pattern, color, and graphics can give direction. The intensity of illumination can guide. Children will tend to move toward the brightest area. Illumination can also influence behavior, particularly if the light intensity is lowered in such areas as coat rooms where the overactive child may cause disruption. Soft light, soft color, and soft textures will tend to calm the children in areas where stimulation and activity are not wanted.

The younger handicapped children may only know two buildings, their home and their school. Many will not have been to a store, an office building, a theatre, or downtown. Those born in cities may never have seen the countryside, rivers, lakes, or farms.

At school they have been launched into a strange world. Textures, finishes, light, and color can help them to orient themselves so they can move through the school complex with assurance and confidence that the environment is friendly.

SAFETY

As noted earlier, if a child is frightened or fearful of hurting himself, he is not receptive to learning. If he is insecure, he will be unwilling and unable to cope with the learning task. Above all, he must enjoy the confidence of security and the assurance that the unexpected will not happen. The designer must foresee and prepare for every emergency. The teacher must do the same. Safety therefore must be a characteristic of the teaching-learning process and foremost in the minds of both the teacher and the architect.

Fire Safety Measures

Fortunately, because of enforced building codes, there have been few tragic fires in school buildings. This must not cause us to rest content that it will not happen. Fire in a school building will always be the greatest predictable danger to the largest number of persons, though earthquake or flood also rank high in certain localities. Adequate provision for the quick and complete evacuation of a school building is imperative in a school for normal children. When the children are handicapped, "adequate provision" is not enough. Special provisions are essential to insure their safety.

Crippled children cannot move rapidly and some of the handicapped pupils at times of crisis will not respond to directions normally or may not respond at all. Many will be confused and frightened, incapable of interpreting directions correctly. Some may be braced in chairs or standing tables while others may be in soundproof rooms out of hearing of the alarm system. Some will be in toilet rooms, others resting in a cot room. We may be sure that all will be disturbed by an alarm, particularly if they have not learned through practice and experience how to reach safety. The teacher must be prepared for all of these contingencies and must know from experience how the children will react, which will be special problems, and which will need the most help.

Since many of the children will react slowly and their response will be unpredictable, normal provisions for safety may not be adequate. Special consideration must be given to the number of exits. Should the number be increased to reduce the travel distance for the severely physically handicapped? Many schools, recognizing the importance of safety, have limited the schools for the handicapped to one story and have provided exits from each classroom. This is not always possible on limited sites, in which case the number of stairways should be increased. When the mobility of the children is far below normal, there is unfortunately no hard and fast rule for this increase; but, if we must judge, it should be on the safe side.

In an integrated school, movement of the normal children may make it difficult for the handicapped to exit safely if the teachers are unable to control the group. The normal children will be stronger. If they panic, the handicapped may suffer. On the other hand, a *buddy system* akin to that used in swimming pools can be of great value.

It is imperative that the children should have fire drills frequently. They must learn to exit together without interference. All children must know where the exits are located. Teachers should know where fire extinguishers are located, and all who are physically able should know how to operate a fire extinguisher. Fire departments will usually be pleased to demonstrate their proper use. Substitute teachers must also be instructed in fire drill procedures, must be ready to carry out the evacuation procedure as efficiently as the regular teacher, and both must emphasize that *all* children be accounted for. Every possible place that a handicapped child may be must be checked to be certain that no one is left in the building. Remember that the impulse of some may be to hide.

When a building is multistoried and elevators are normally used by the children and staff, all must understand that elevators will cease to operate if there is a power failure unless they are served by the emergency power system and the system operates properly. If they are not, use of the elevators may trap children and staff between floors if the power goes off. An elevator shaft has all of the characteristics of a chimney when there is a fire on lower floors.

The normal fire alarm will be an audible gong. The alarm system should be extended to sound proof or sound treated rooms such as the speech therapy rooms to insure that all children able to hear will be warned. The normal fire alarm system will serve all but the deaf. Since they will not hear the alarm, the system must be supplemented by the addition of flashing lights at critical points where the deaf children will see them.

Normally, we are satisfied when we have made adequate provision for egress from a building, but with handicapped children our planning must proceed beyond getting them out of the building. Where normal children can run across the grass, children in wheelchairs cannot. Their route must be paved. Where normal children can step up or down curbs, children in wheelchairs cannot. In panic they may upset. All curbs that are part of escape routes should be rolled. Every evacuation plan must insure that the escape route will adequately serve the children who may be required to use it, even when they are excited and fearful.

Schools in cold climates have the additional problem of determining where children can go when a building is evacuated. Is a warm shelter available for those who did not have time to put on coats? If shelter is not available, what provision can be made to care for those who must stay warm? Are the heated school buses quickly available? Are adjacent homes available? Should the heat lamps of the arrival-departure area be put on the emergency power system? Should there be a supply of blankets conveniently near? Each school must find its own answers and be ready.

Safe Movement in the Building

Children moving through corridors unaccompanied are particularly susceptible to hazardous situations. Generally, doors open into rooms, but classroom doors opening into corridors should open against a wall to eliminate the hazard of upsetting a child. An open door should never reduce the width of the corridor. Building codes will generally not permit sliding doors as access to escape corridors, but they can significantly reduce hazards when used on both built-in and movable cabinets.

It is advisable to eliminate door closers in schools for the handicapped. While they conveniently close the door, they also make the door more difficult to open. Some children will not have sufficient strength. When a door closes automatically, children may be frightened by having the door close on their fingers. The pressure will not hurt them, but the experience will not be helpful.

When visibility through a door is essential for safety and glass is used in the door or in the panel beside the door, the glass should be either wire glass or unbreakable. The local building code will usually govern the area of glass in doors or walls if they are a part of the emergency escape path since glass does not resist extreme heat. Failure of a glass wall will destroy the safety of the escape corridor.

Blind children must be particularly careful in corridors, and everyone must be mindful of their handicap. No movable furniture should ever be permitted in a corridor, nor should any piece of equipment be allowed to stand temporarily in the corridor. Built-in furniture should not reduce the width of a corridor, and all tripping hazards should be eliminated.

When planning a school that will serve blind children, corridor widths should be constant, not wider in one place and narrower in another. An exception is those areas deliberately planned to simulate problems for mobility training. Double swinging doors in corridors should be avoided. Alcoves that create corners should be avoided where possible or reduced to a minimum. Ideally, all corners would be rounded, but this is not always possible.

Blind children will quickly learn the pattern of corridors and related rooms, but some aids are desirable. Floor textures and wall textures can serve to warn of a change in direction. This is essential at the top of stairs. Changes of direction can be signaled by a current of air from a fan or the sound of a ticking clock. A change in ceiling height will normally modify sound and signal a change.

Many schools provide an emergency call button in each teaching area to allow the teacher to call for assistance without leaving the room. An audible call system is equally effective. If there are rooms in which a physically handicapped child may be working alone, consideration should be given to an emergency call system operable by a child lying or crawling on the floor. When he is unable to get up after falling, an emergency call button three feet above the floor may be beyond his reach!

Calls for assistance will generally go to the office or the switchboard where it is imperative to have a directory of hospitals, an ambulance service, and a telephone number for the personal physician of each child.

At many points within a building there are very hot pipes that are either a part of the heating system or the hot water system. Where these are accessible to children, the latter must be protected. Ideally, each system would be designed with the hazard in mind so that none of the hot piping would be accessible. When pipe is visible, however, dangerously hot and safely cold can be distinguished by color: red or yellow for hot, blue or green for cold. Hot water lines serving lavatories should be high enough to be above the legs of children in wheelchairs or covered with insulation to preclude burning the leg of a child who may have no feeling in one or both legs. Other exposed hot lines that are normally a part of a heating system should be insulated in the same way. Some types of cast-iron radiators will get hotter than desirable if an automatic system calls for more heat on a very cold day. If cast-iron radiators have to be used, consideration should be given to enclosing them in cabinets even though doing so reduces their efficiency.

Sharp edges and corners are an increasing hazard because of the more common use of plastic laminate for the finished surface of cabinets, casework, and tables. The plastic laminate is a thin hard layer resistant to soil and damage. When the layers meet at an edge or a corner, the joint, even though slightly beveled, is square and sharp. The hazard can be reduced somewhat by rounding the exposed corners or using a bumper type rounded edge, but this is often not possible or too expensive. When this type of corner is necessary, it would be better to accept a less durable or resistant surface and eliminate the sharp corner or edge.

Knobs, levers, thermostats, and other types of controls normally project from walls and are consequently hazardous. If they cannot be eliminated or recessed, they can at least be grouped high enough on a wall so that the danger of falling against them is minimal. Whenever possible, knobs on doors and drawers should be eliminated in favor of a recessed pull with no projection.

Projections from a wall are particularly dangerous in a gymnasium where children may be moving rapidly with their attention concentrated on a ball or another person. There should be a warning carpet belt around the perimeter of the playing floor for the partially sighted. Walls can be padded in critical areas. If a projecting device cannot be eliminated, it should be located above head level or protected by a screen.

When study areas or other spaces, enclosed carrells, toilet stalls, or isolation rooms, are designed for occupancy by one child, any lock that can be controlled on the inside must be unlockable from the outside. If a child is unable or unwilling to unlock a door and no provision has been made to do so from the outside, the only alternative is to remove the door by taking it off its hinges. This can be done if the hinges are accessible. If they are not accessible, the door or wall must be broken. Should a child be unable to open a door because he has fainted or fallen and cannot get up, the time element may be critical.

Preferably, glass should not be used at heights against which a child can fall. If, however, vision panels in or beside doors are considered necessary, the glass should be either nonbreakable tempered glass or wire glass. Either type will give adequate protection to the child. The Fire Department may have to break the glass used in exterior doors to enter the school when it is closed. This glass should always be wire glass, because it is breakable.

Building codes will require the provision of an emergency generator to furnish power for certain lights and equipment necessary during an evacuation of the building. This system will illuminate corridors and exit signs. It should also operate all elevators to preclude children or staff being trapped in an elevator if the power fails.

SELF-CARE

A major objective of education is to provide children with the skills and knowledge necessary to a full, independent life. Normally, children would be expected to learn toileting, bathing, and self-care skills at home. However, when the rate of learning is slowed by limited experience or by physical or mental deficits or by other factors in the home situation, education in all of its aspects, including self-care, must be promoted during school hours.

Lance and Koch [102] studied the responses of 107 parents of young handicapped children (60 of the children having two or three handicaps) to questions about the importance of learning and the difficulty of teaching four self-help activities: toileting, eating, dressing and washing, and grooming skill. Parents' responses were used to develop instructional materials useful at home. In such instances, teachers and parents work cooperatively as self-help educators.

This learning process must be included in schooling as a continuing experience. Put another way, the school must make positive provision for self-care instruction whenever the child's need and desire provides a teaching opportunity, at any age or at all ages. To do this requires modification of the physical characteristics of the teaching space as well as an enlargement of educational objectives to include self-care skills. It must mirror our concern for the *whole* child which is so essential in a learning program for the handicapped.

Personal Grooming Skills

The school will have as many opportunities as the home to at least teach children dressing skills necessary for normal overgarments, hats, coats, sweaters, and shoes. If the children can participate in the recess periods for outdoor relaxation, they may put on overcoats four or five times a day. If lavatories, mirrors, and toilets are in the same general area as clothes storage, the school can teach and supervise the development of essential grooming skills as well, repeating them each day until the child is independent.

Storage of Clothing

For clothes storage, the standard type of metal school locker is not only unnecessary but undesirable. In the first place, it is a strange piece of equipment with a sliding latch that is usually difficult and often impossible for handicapped children to operate. In the second place, learning to use a locker has little relation to self-care when the child has yet to learn how to hang his coat on a coat hanger, and, in turn, hang the coat hanger on a rod or hook. When the older child develops sufficient skill to promise employment opportunity, he then needs to be taught the use of the normal locker he will probably encounter in an employee's locker room. But this should be a part of his vocational preparation which is discussed elsewhere, not a part of his first learning experiences. First, he must learn what to do at home. Later, he may learn what to do at work.

At selected places in the school, depending on whether there is a single coat room or many different coat rooms, provision should be made for spare clothing; sweaters if it turns cold, boots if it rains, slippers for indoor wear, and extra underclothes for toileting accidents. This storage area with individual cubicles can also serve as a place for each child's grooming articles; his comb, hair brush, tooth brush, tooth paste, nail file, wash cloth and towel, as well as a mat and light blanket for use during rest periods. Ideally, each child should have his own cubicle, a hanging space, and a classwork space marked with a changeable nameplate. If he has not reached the stage of learning to read, he can use a symbol substitute for his name. A full-length mirror conveniently nearby will help him develop self-awareness and teach him proper dress.

Hanging rods must be reachable from wheel chairs, or preferably, not more than 48 inches above the floor. Coat pegs can be at 30 inches and 42 inches. Storage cubicles can be the open pigeonhole type or drawers; but, if the latter are used, they must be easily operable on ball bearing tracks with drawer pulls that are easily controllable by children unable to grasp a knob.

The dressing and care of children require teachers to consume considerable time and energy. They are teaching the skills that each child must develop. The convenience and effectiveness of this kind of teaching space can accelerate the child's progress and reduce the teacher's task if those responsible for the planning are thoughtful. The design can encourage children to help themselves, if they can reach and operate everything they are taught to use. Space should permit the children to help each other. There can be a mistaken tendency in planning to minimize dressing space in favor of other teaching space, and to overlook the importance of teaching self-care. Each child must learn to dress and undress, to manage buttons, snaps, zippers, belts, shoes, socks, and shoe laces. The teacher needs space in order to teach these skills.

Boots are usually dirty, and provision for them is best provided by a low shelf, often below the coat hanging space. A shelf of wire mesh will hold the boots but let the dirt drop through to the floor for easy cleaning. In order to put on shoes or boots, the pupil will need something to sit on. A built-in bench is desirable.

When schools are located in cold damp climates, provision is often made for the drying of wet clothes in a heated, ventilated cabinet or dryer. This may also serve to provide dry warm bath towels for the incontinent children who have accidents that require cleanup.

Facilities for Grooming

The child who is ambulatory will normally not have a major problem with wash sinks provided that their height is suited to the child's height. But children confined to wheelchairs have no opportunity to learn grooming skills unless the sink is open underneath at a height that is related to the height of the wheelchair seat and has reachable control valves. Children under five in *Little Tot* wheelchairs will need to have the sink height at not more than 26½ inches. Some sinks should be set at 31½ inches and others at 33½ inches. Their height will allow the arms of standard size wheelchairs to pass under the sink so that the child is close to the bowl. In this regard, a special sink is made that is physically thin and 24 inches from front to back. It is cantilevered from the wall and provides more leg room underneath so that a seated person can be closer to the bowl. This is excellent for adults, but it is too deep from front to back for children to reach the control valves conveniently. Surgical type wrist control valves may allow children with arm and hand involvement to control the water more easily, but these are not recommended because they are *special*. While it may be more difficult, the children should learn to use the control valves they will normally encounter.

Mirrors at wash basins should be positioned to permit children in wheelchairs to see themselves. They may be in the plane of the wall if the lower edge can be close to the level of the sink, or they may slope outward by setting the upper edge a few inches from the wall. If older boys are to be taught to use electric razors, an electric receptacle should be near, low, and reachable.

A typical medicine cabinet cannot be reached by a child in a wheelchair and may even be difficult for an adult. While the mirror should be behind a wash basin, a medicine cabinet that is independent of the mirror can be at any reachable location, often an intersecting wall adjacent to the wash basin. While a medicine cabinet is not normal in a school toilet room, one or more should be located in positions that will allow the teacher to demonstrate their use.

If children in wheelchairs are taught to wash their hair, they will be able to use the sink more conveniently if a horizontal grab bar is installed on the wall behind and above the sink but below the mirror. This allows those who have the strength to pull themselves up from the chair seat to a more convenient position for rinsing.

Drinking Facilities

Drinking fountains are not convenient to children in wheelchairs since the fountains can normally only be approached from the side. They will be usable to all, however, if a paper cup dispenser and disposal cabinet are within easy reach.

Toileting Adjustments

It must be remembered that many physically handicapped children are not the normal size for their age. Their physical dimensions are usually smaller. Young adults are not necessarily adult size, and a five year old child may measure smaller than a normal three year old. Children with spina bifida are always shorter in the legs and trunk, and many children have bent or collapsed trunks. Some will have no arms. Some may have no legs. Some may have both artificial arms and artificial legs.

Consequently, the problems of toileting are magnified when we seek solutions that will encourage children to learn to take care of themselves. Those with minimal involvement will have few problems. The other extreme will be the small, frail, armless child who will always need assistance. Between these extremes will be degrees of handicaps that make it imperative to provide varied schemes for the design of the toilet fixture and its *helps*.

For best physiological function, the correct position on the toilet is with the legs apart and the feet flat on the floor or a platform. Ideally, for the handicapped child, the buttocks should be well supported by the sides and back of the seat. The domestic type tank toilet provides back support, but the normal institutional toilet with a flush valve and no tank will require some modification for children needing back support.

The height of the toilet seat must vary if children can be taught to transfer from a wheelchair. There are three heights of toilets normally available: (1) the junior size with a seat approximately 12 inches high, (2) the normal toilet which has a seat approximately 15 inches high, and (3) the special height toilets of 20 inches for adults using an adult size wheelchair. While transfer is easier from a wheelchair seat that is the same height as a toilet seat, this usually does not allow the feet to be placed flat on the floor, or at times, even to reach the floor. Consequently, the child does not have the security and confidence he should have during what is inevitably a period of stress and concern. Again, a fixed or movable platform is desirable as a foot rest.

If the school program is designed to serve infants and the very young, it will have to provide space in the toileting areas for *pot* training in small chairs. While disposable *pot* linings are available, a clinical sink with spray should be provided. This will also serve for the disposal of bedpans needed by children confined to a litter or bed. A convenient bedpan washer-sterilizer should be provided that includes rack storage if different children are to use the same bedpans.

Unfortunately, there is not a sufficient variety of toilet seats to meet all handicapped children's needs. The split bumper seat with an open front is the most hygienic and easily cleaned. The size of the hole, however, is too wide to hold children with a small buttocks. Children can and have fallen through. The open front eliminates a possible hand hold often necessary to maintain balance if a grab bar is not within reach. On the other hand, the open front permits more convenient insertion of a suppository for children who require it. This problem must be reviewed in detail in order to arrive at an acceptable solution. Some kind of adapter is inevitable, because no seat on today's market will suit all children.

The seated child must be able to reach the flushing device easily. If not, the toilet will not be flushed until the teacher arrives. Unfortunately, the normal institutional flushing valve behind the seat encourages the child to avoid flushing because he cannot reach it. The additional expense of placing the flushing valve beside the toilet rather than behind it is worth it.

While privacy is desirable, many handicaps do not permit a child to use the normal toilet stall with the usual narrow door. Even if the stall is larger, children in wheelchairs cannot use it. Privacy can be provided by ceiling hung curtains on curtain tracks or by alcoves within the toilet rooms. Since some children on litters must use a bedpan, the toilet room must be large enough to accommodate the litter and an aide; again, a curtain can provide the desirable privacy. There must also be sufficient space for the person giving assistance during the learning process.

Within a school where the children are learning for living, there must be basically three categories of toilets, and each has its own peculiar problems. First, there must be the normal toilet for children who can learn to use it. Second, there must be a toilet for children in wheelchairs or litters. This will require both ample space for turning the wheelchair and grab bar aides for children learning to transfer. Third, there must be a toilet with a convenient and available counter and sink for the cleanup of children who are incontinent, not toilet trained, or who have toileting accidents. These children will usually be smaller, and the counter should be long enough to lay them horizontally for more convenient dressing and undressing. The counter will be cold, so storage for towel cover is essential. Clean clothes must be available, and often a small laundry room with washer and dryer is necessary, depending on the frequency of this type of care. The desirability of warm towels has already been mentioned, and a heat lamp will help when children are frail and the room is cool.

Some schools have provided each kind of toilet accommodation in each toilet area. Some have provided *cleanup toilets* only to serve the lower grades. They are directly accessible from the classroom because small children should not be out of sight in toilet areas. It would only encourage accidents. Some schools have provided separate individual toilet areas for each of the three types of toileting problem. In the design of new facilities, the scheme for toileting will depend on the size of the school, the distance to toilet areas from classroom areas, and the generosity of the budget. Prior to planning, the architect and the teachers should be in agreement on the toileting scheme. There is more than one answer.

If the school accommodates children from nursery school to high school, it must provide urinals at usable heights, lowest for the small children and normal heights for adult size boys. Again, the flushing device must be reachable, preferably at the side rather than above and out of the reach of smaller children.

When normal toilet partitions are provided, it is desirable to make minor modifications. If a latch is included, it should be operable from the outside in case of emergency. Hyperactive and mentally retarded children may be expected to swing on the doors. Therefore, hinges should be heavy-duty and the partitions firmly attached to both floor and ceiling. Ceiling hung partitions should be avoided because they are not sufficiently rigid.

Because mentally retarded or other handicapped children are curious, toilet partitions may start closer to the floor and be higher than normal to discourage looking under or over.

Needless to say, grab bars for pulling and pushing should be provided at toilets. They will require steel plates within the walls for secure anchoring. Even the toilet paper holder should be securely anchored because, in an emergency, it may be used as a grab bar. Shower curtains and towel bars may also be used for support. Likewise, sinks must have more than normal support. They have to resist the load of adult size heavy children on crutches who need to lean on them when using them.

Facilities for Bathing

While facilities for bathing are not commonly provided in regular day schools, there may be instances when the *activities for daily living* instruction must include both a shower and a tub. Since the children should learn to use normal accommodations, one shower stall can be of normal dimensions. If a second can be provided, it should be large enough for a wheelchair and should have a floor ridge at the entrance rather than a curb. There will probably be an abnormal amount of water on the bathroom floor, making a floor drain essential. Shower controls should be within easy reach of a child seated in a wheelchair and may be located outside the stall. In schools, it is imperative to provide thermostatic control of all hot water to insure that it is never hot enough to be harmful.

For instructional purposes, the bath tub will have to be a normal tub, but it can illustrate the use of grab bars that could be installed at home. The location of grab bars for the physically handicapped would be suited for each individual. But the school tub will have to serve as a teaching device for different physical deficits. Therefore, it would be desirable to locate a vertical grab bar near the center of the tub and horizontal bars about 3 inches above the tub along the wall side and the end opposite the controls. If the controls are placed at the center of the long dimension of the tub and 8 inches above the edge, a child can usually bathe without more assistance than is necessary to get into or out of the tub. If, on the other hand, the tub is not used for teaching but to serve the convenience of an aide who is bathing the child, it should either be high enough to require minimal stooping or have a pit along one side in which the aide can stand.

Feeding One's Self

Instruction in self-feeding must be provided for many handicapped pupils to supplement home training in many cases. For those children who have difficulty grasping, the occupational therapist may devise grasping aids, but the practicum of self-feeding should take place in the dining area. Where physical involvement is severe to the possible embarrassment of the child, consideration should be given to a special *learning* dining area with a mirrored wall for self-observation.

Many schools which include handicapped students have found cafeteria service entirely satisfactory for the majority of the children particularly if the system serves made-up trays. However, some will be incapable of moving through a cafeteria line and must be served. This provides an opportunity for older, less handicapped or non-handicapped children to help others, and to develop their sense of usefulness and responsibility.

Food Preparation

The use of a kitchen and its normal equipment is certainly one aspect of self-care. Development of the skill to prepare food is essential to every independent person. However, the place and manner in which instruction is given may vary. The minimum requirement would be an ordinary kitchen similar to a home kitchen but large enough for a small group of children. The principal objective would be safety training and the performance of simple food preparation and kitchen tasks. Equipment would include a sink, disposal, gas or electric stove or possibly both, a refrigerator, dishwasher, trash basket, clock, cabinets and cupboards with all the utensils, and dishes and flatware necessary for an introduction to food preparation skills.

The optimum area for all children, handicapped or not, would be a complete home economics suite with all of the above, plus areas for sewing, laundry, and homecare. This will be discussed in a later section on the development of vocational skills.

Just as instruction in toileting must continue in school, grooming that normally would be taught at home should be reinforced with further instruction. At some point in each teaching-learning area, equipment should be provided to make this possible. A full-length mirror is desirable, but a three-way full-length mirror would be better. Many children have never seen themselves in a side view. A white porcelain sink rather than grey stainless steel will encourage tooth brushing and hand scrubbing. When the white sink is flushed and cleaned, the result is obvious. Eye, ear, and nose care can be emphasized without special equipment, but shoe polishing will require storage and some kind of protection for clothes.

While not necessary in each teaching-learning area, a beauty parlor area will stimulate the older girls and even long haired boys! It should be equipped as a normal beauty parlor with shampoo sinks, hair dryers, manicurist table, and the other necessary professional tools and supplies to encourage self care and possibly stimulate vocational interest.

CHAPTER VIII

PUPILS AND THE BUILDING

THIS CHAPTER IS intended to illustrate some relationships between some of the school activities in which exceptional children may engage and certain elements of the school building. The examples were chosen to be as general as possible. Thus, they deal with flooring, walls, doors, windows, hand railings and other wall attached items, and storage space, so far as the building is concerned. The pupil activities include ordinary movement in the building, use of crutches and wheel chairs, behavior during anger or frustration or tantrums, normal curiosity reactions, and extemporaneous play.

What follows should not be taken as a list of prescriptions. Rather, it is a group of examples of the kinds of items which need to be referred to in the educational program, and specifications which need to be discussed fully by the design team before design and materials decisions are made.

INFLUENCE OF BUILDING DETAILS ON THE LEARNING ENVIRONMENT

Normal criteria for the design and construction of school buildings are adequately covered in many excellent books and professional journals. These are easily available to all who are interested. Schools must be structurally sound, built of materials and equipment that have long life under conditions of heavy usage.

These general criteria apply equally to schools for handicapped children. But this is not enough. The handicapped child has special problems. His mobility and dexterity may be limited. His sight and learning may be impaired. His emotional stability may be limited. His mental development may be below normal. All of these deficits must be recognized in any consideration of general criteria to insure that each child can perform to the limits of his capability. The building must not get in the way! The building should not create hazards that may hurt the child. (You may be sure, however, that the children will create hazards that may hurt the building!)

Whether the project is new construction or the remodeling of existing space, special attention must be given to all of the details that can minimize or eliminate the many problems created by physical, mental, and emotional deficits. For example, when a school accommodates handicapped children, it must be decided to either discipline the child or allow the building to be damaged. Slamming a door or smashing a thermostat are great ways to relieve tension and frustration. A skilled teacher will normally avoid the discipline and accept the damage. Punishment is seldom acceptable in the educational program, and this challenge to the designer cannot be avoided. *The child is important. The building is not.*

Floor Surface Considerations

The ideal floor surface should be nonslip, reasonably smooth, preferably resilient, not too resistant to wheeled carts and wheelchairs, and easily cleaned. Rubber tile meets all of these requirements, and even though it is thin, it has some resilience to cushion a fall. Vinyl asbestos tile is equally effective provided that it is not waxed and buffed to a high slippery sheen. Cork has been used and is particularly effective in cushioning a fall. It is nonslip, reasonably easy to care for, and long lasting as long as heels are flat. Women's spiked heels were fashionable a few years ago and, if styles run in cycles, may be fashionable again. They marked resilient tile, and they were particularly damaging to cork.

Terrazzo, a material created by imbedding marble chips in wet concrete and grinding it smooth when dry, is an excellent material and extensively used in institutional buildings where the budget will permit it. The resulting surface is long lasting, resistant to wear, easily cleaned, visually attractive, and water resistant. However, if it is used where there are children on crutches or canes, it is extremely slippery and hazardous when wet.

Carpet has proven an excellent material for teaching-learning areas and has been used in corridors. To reduce its resistance to the wheels of carts, litters, and wheelchairs, it is best to omit the cushion underlayment and attach the carpet directly to the concrete floor slab. The carpet should be a hard twist weave rather than a cut or looped pile, again to provide a harder surface for children of limited strength confined to wheelchairs.

The trend to carpeted floors in teaching-learning areas and the consequent increase in the children's use of the floor to sit at work or play may require consideration of the temperature of the floor surface. Cold floors will encourage incontinence in children who have problems of bladder control. Then, too, a cold floor is not a healthy floor for frail children who are susceptible to chilling.

If the school floor is on earth, as it would normally be in a one-story building, and the school is in a cold climate, the floor should be insulated. The method of doing so will vary with location and the materials commonly available.

Of course, the floors may be heated as a part of a radiant heating system for the building, but, if the provision of radiant heat in selected areas requires a separate and different heating system than the remainder of the building, the additional cost of the separate system may not be acceptable.

When children are partially sighted or blind, the changing texture of floors can help to identify travel patterns through the school and in the playground areas. The kind of texture is of no significance, only the texture change that identifies a direction change or a warning. This is particularly essential if the school is more than one story and requires partially sighted or blind children to be warned when approaching a stairway. The change of texture should occur at both the top and bottom to clearly define the beginning and end of the run of stairs. Normally, a change of texture is not necessary at intermediate landings since the stair hand rail will guide a child from one stair run to another. Needless to say, the hand rail at the wall should be continuous around the intermediate landings.

When changes of floor materials are desirable at the thresholds of doorways, every effort must be made to reduce or eliminate tripping hazards. A typical child may easily step on or over them. A physically handicapped child, who is able only to shuffle his feet may not make it.

It is not always possible to eliminate slight changes because of the additional expense of pouring the finished concrete floor to varying levels. It is normal to recess the concrete slab to receive ceramic tile or quarry tile or to provide for recessed door mats at entrances. It is not normal to recess a floor slab to receive carpet because it cannot be considered permanent. Areas carpeted today may not be carpeted tomorrow. When there is a change from a hard surface to a carpeted surface, the normal metal edge strip for carpet has been an acceptable solution.

When floors must be water resistant, they will generally be finished in ceramic materials. If a floor is waterproof, the corollary follows that it will retain water. If there is a curb, such as there may be at an individual shower stall or a gang shower, the possible depth of the water retained will equal the height of the curb. Children sometimes discover that they can turn on the shower, put a wash cloth or towel over the floor drain, and create a pool! In the case of a gang shower, the pool can be large enough to encourage a group of children in vigorous water play. A shower stall is normally made water tight with a lead or copper pan under the floor whose edges turn up the wall a few inches. To preclude damage to the wall when the stall is used as a pool, the edges of the pan should extend at least twelve inches higher than the height of the curb.

There will be areas within a school where floors must be grease-proof, (food service) and others that must be resistant to solvents (shops and garages). None of these areas are peculiar to schools for the handicapped or present any problems that warrant discussion here.

Wall Construction

The type of wall construction will generally be determined by cost. This will vary in different localities and climates, so general statements are meaningless. There are no problems of any consequence created by different types of wall construction, though some types of interior partitions have secondary advantages. For instance, if interior partitions are finished in what is normally called *drywall,* a prefabricated gypsum board attached to wood or metal studs, and if the drywall is covered with a vinyl wall covering instead of paint, all walls so constructed are usable as tackboards. They are not as resistant to sound transmission but considerably less expensive than mounting an equivalent area of tackboard on a heavier partition.

Interior partitions and doorways are particularly vulnerable to damage. Many children will be moving about in wheelchairs, litters, carts, tricycles, and even beds. The drivers of these vehicles are novices. Some do not have either the skill or the strength to adequately control a wheeled vehicle. As a result, pedals and axles will gouge the plaster, slash the vinyl wall covering, or chip away the paint. Most vehicles are provided with bumpers or covers on the parts most liable to damage walls, but, as the vehicles age, the protective devices seem to disappear and damage begins.

Damage to the walls of corridors will vary inversely as the width of the corridor. When the width is 7 feet or less, a considerable amount of damage may be expected. When corridors reach 10 feet in width or wider, damage will be minimal.

Since most of the damage to walls will occur in the lower 3 feet, protection can be provided by a wainscot of material sufficiently resistant to impact, scraping, and cutting. Heavy duty vinyl fabrics are sometimes used but are vulnerable to tearing and not easily repaired after the damage is done. Ceramic tile and resilient floor tile are effective wainscot materials. Panels of plastic laminate materials are effective, easily maintained, but generally more expensive. When corridor floors are carpeted, the carpet can be carried up the wall with the edge securely fastened. Whatever the material may be, it must resist the tendency of inquisitive hyperactive children to determine whether it can be removed.

At intersecting corridors, corners are most vulnerable and securely anchored cover guards are essential. These may be metal or plastic. Clear plastic is often used over decorative wall covering. Opaque plastic can be used where appearance is not critical.

Doors

Damage to doors will also be inversely proportional to their width. An adult size wheelchair will go thru a 30-inch wide doorway but with only an inch to spare on either side. At this width, considerable damage may be expected both to the edge of the door and to the metal frame in which it is installed.

The door can be protected in different ways. If it is wood, a metal angle of aluminum or stainless steel can be inset in the lower section of the exposed edge, or a plastic cover may be used to protect the entire exposed edge of the door. If this method is used, the hinge must be adjusted to accommodate the cover. A third method uses what are called offset hinges. These permit the door to swing back so that the edge of the door is not exposed. The metal frame of the door then takes the damage. A fourth method uses metal doors or doors covered on all surfaces with plastic laminate. The latter are practically indestructible and retain their appearance for many years.

There seems to be no way to protect the painted surface of the metal frame (door buck) surrounding a door. Paint will be scraped off if the doorway is narrow, but it seems that an equal amount of damage is done when the door is wider. The skillful, precise control of a wheelchair or other wheeled vehicles is not common to handicapped children, as has been noted earlier. Consequently, damage cannot be avoided. One school administrator pointed out that the solution lay in accepting the damage where damage seemed minimal and repainting or touching up the door buck every six months.

Not only the door, but the entire doorway is vulnerable if not properly installed. A door is normally hung on a metal frame called a door buck. This frame is installed in the wall when the wall is built. At that time, it is firmly anchored to the wall materials which could be tile, concrete block, metal studs, or wood studs. The material of the wall, at this point, is not important, but its resistance to impact can be critical. Hyperactive children often find that slamming a door is a convenient way to relieve their frustration. Because of the leverage provided by the hinged connection to the door buck, and because doors are usually wider than normal, a considerable force can be generated. If the door buck is not securely anchored to the adjoining wall, the floor, and the underside of the floor or roof above, even a relatively small child can generate enough force to move or twist the door buck, break the anchoring, and severely damage surrounding plaster.

Wherever possible, doors should open against an adjoining wall where the swing of the door may be stopped with a floor bumper that does not create a tripping hazard. Avoid the type of bumper that is mounted on the adjoining wall at the height of the door knob. The leverage of the door makes it simple for children to drive the door knob and the bumper back thru the normal plaster wall!

Door closers are sometimes essential, but, when they are used, it should be recognized that weaker children may not have the strength to operate them or even to resist them when the door is closing. Fingers caught will not normally be hurt, but the experience will be frightening. If doors must close automatically but slowly, it is possible to use a gravity hinge. When the door is opened, it rises slightly on a sloping plane of the hinge. When released, gravity closes it. The gravity hinge is common on toilet compartment doors but can also be used on larger doors. Since the weight of the door resists its movement, more strength is required to operate it.

Where door closers are not required but some resistance to a full swing is desirable, an adjustable hold open device can be built into the top of the door. When this is installed and the friction adjusted, the door will stay where it happens to be when released. This device operates properly when used with standard hinges. However, it should not be used if the door is hung on offset hinges. The combination of the offset hinge leverage and the holdopen device restraint at the top of the door creates a pattern of forces that can tear the door buck out of the wall. The force has to be abnormal, but when it happens, the only way to repair the damage is to demolish the adjacent wall and rebuild it.

Windows

If children are expected to be provided operable windows, the operating mechanism must be within the reach of a child in a wheelchair. This means that it must be low and directly accessible. There should be no cabinets between the window and the child. The trend toward air conditioned schools simplifies the window problem, and the preference for the constancy and adequacy of artificial lighting diminishes the need for large areas of glass. Some schools have been built and enthusiastically accepted with no windows whatsoever in the teaching-learning areas.

Wall-Attached Items

There will always be a necessity for wall supports. Grab bars are a typical example. There are also other items attached to walls that may not be designed as supports but serve that purpose in emergency situations. A slipping or falling child will grab for the nearest device he can reach. It may be the toilet paper holder, the paper towel holder, a towel bar, or even a shower curtain. To minimize the seriousness of accidents, all of them must first be well built to resist unusual strain and, above all, must be firmly attached. It is not enough to simply attach them to a plaster wall without first providing a metal plate behind the plaster that is securely fastened to the structure. This provides secure attachment that will hold the weight of an adult size child.

Many handicapped children will have to lean on something when they stand. They will lean on a sink, a table top or a cabinet, a chalk tray or the arm of a seat. In many instances, the need for support will be a load of abnormal magnitude, particularly if the child is adult size. Whenever this occurs adequate support, normally a leg of some kind, must be given. A cantilevered sink or table or cabinet top is an invitation to accidents. The same will apply to wall bracketed light fixtures that are within reach. The time will surely come when a child reaching for support will tear them down. A lavatory gooseneck spout and wrist control valves are both vulnerable to damage.

Ventilator Grilles

Inquisitive children will often experiment by stuffing things into places that are not meant to receive things. This is not a trait peculiar to handicapped children but definitely more common. Many pieces of equipment, particularly heating or ventilating units, require grilles. Pieces of fixed equipment sometimes cannot be set flush against walls, and small spaces are left behind them. If material stuffed into grilles or behind equipment will affect their efficient operation, they should be protected by placing a fine screen behind the grille or a closure cover between the equipment and the wall. Light fixtures must not provide a *basket* for things to be thrown into.

Storage Areas

Storage within a school is always a problem and invariably inadequate. First, storage for each teacher, including a lockable unit for a purse and personal items is essential. Storage space for portable or wheeled teaching equipment should be lockable to preclude theft. This is particularly true in the open plan school where a single space without lockable doors may contain many valuable pieces of equipment.

Many building codes require the space where supplies are stored to have an automatic sprinkler system. This is an excellent regulation, but, since planned storage space is often inadequate, spaces not originally intended for storage are so used. The designer can help this situation by avoiding the provision for *convenient* storage places. But if it is necessary to convert space to storage, adequate fire protection should be provided simultaneously. Storage at the lowest floor of stair towers is a prime offender and should never be permitted.

Acoustics

All groups of exceptional children have much to gain from improvements in the acoustical properties of school space. Blind children must rely heavily on accurate hearing. For hearing-handicapped children, the better the acoustics, the better use they can make of hearing aids. Retarded children and youngsters with learning disabilities often suffer from faulty auditory perception, a condition which can be aggravated by real acoustic distortions and inconsistencies. Speech handicapped pupils use the sounds of their voices and other voices to monitor the correctness of their own articulation. Correct auditory feedback is vital in that case. And some children with neurological damage, emotional disorders, or social behavioral limitations are triggered into uncontrolled behavior by excessive or unusual sounds. Therefore, important as excellent acoustics can be to teaching and learning in general, it is of special importance for exceptional children.

The binaural hearing sense can enable blind and partially seeing children to identify and concentrate attention on what they need to hear and to ignore much unwanted sound. It can be of special importance in discriminating against noise. Use of the binaural sense in an architectural setting can help the listener establish the location of sound source. It can also help to give a feeling for the size and shape of a room when the same information is not available through vision. High quality acoustics, therefore, has increased value for pupils who are blind or have very limited sight.

The recent trend toward providing large multipurpose spaces for instruction brought acoustic problems with it. The rectangular classroom with high ceilings, though otherwise less desirable, constituted space with excellent potential for high quality acoustics. Excellence in acoustics is more difficult to achieve in relatively open areas where the total air volume may be divided into several connecting regions. Coupled air spaces in that setting and in other imaginative designs offer challenging problems to the architect. These include the exclusion of undesirable echoing, strong reflections, focusing, disturbing diffraction effects, dead spaces, and unequal sound distribution. And that must be accomplished in the context of a steadily increasing noise level in all communities.

A 1972 study has concluded that jet noise at fifteen Los Angeles area schools is creating two serious issues. It hinders education, and it may be causing permanent damage to students.

The sound penetrates the schools, resulting in high enough noise levels to disrupt learning tasks every two minutes. School nurses at one of the schools have found some hearing loss in virtually all the children. Youngsters also appear to become abnormal in their emotional responses and vocal behavior, and there is an unusually high incidence of fights and traumatic responses among the school children.

The study was conducted by William C. Meecham and is reported in brief in *Education U.S.A.*[116] It seems advisable, certainly, to guard against noise pollution either by judicious site selection or by soundproofing.

There are some circumstances in which ambient noise should be kept even below usually accepted levels. Joan Fassler has found that certain cerebral palsied children changed from grades of failure to grades of passing when the auditory input conditions were reduced by putting sound mufflers over the children's ears. There was no similar effect with nonhandicapped pupils.[64]

In later studies, Fassler found also that disturbed children, most of whom had been diagnosed as autistic or psychotic, gave significantly greater attention to school tasks under conditions of reduced auditory stimulation. In a number of instances, the children continued voluntarily to use sound mufflers on their ears after Fassler's experiment was concluded.[65, 66]

Lighting

Since lighting is one of the dominant elements that conveys the feeling of what a place is like, it should be used as a special instrument of environmental manipulation.

Successful overall effect requires the introduction of light sources at various heights. Drop lights, desk lights, and lights under shelves can give uninteresting spaces variation in tone and identity. Moreover, they give the individual the opportunity for some degree of control over his own micro surroundings. And since schools provide few such opportunities, each of them assumes a special significance.

Wiring delivered down from the ceiling tends to be less expensive and less in the path of floor cleaning or traffic. But unless it is well handled, it can be visually distracting. Installations that have been integrated with other ceiling functions of lighting and air handling and that have had appropriate down-delivery hardware, prove to be capable and unobtrusive.

CHAPTER IX

PLANNING THE SPECIAL EDUCATION FACILITY

DESIGNING SCHOOLS AND SCHOOLING

DESIGNING IS PLANNING that meets specific needs. It must often be original, especially when the need is new or has not been previously *designed for*. Designing, however, is not usually completely original; most often, a new design is adapted from previously known designs. When seen this way, it is plain that teachers *design* as part of their daily plans. The process the professional designer uses is closely akin to the process used by a teacher who plans how and under what conditions certain teaching will be done, how learning will take place, or what form a certain curriculum will take.

The process of designing schools and schooling is an activity focused on the interface between instruction and space. It begins with the teacher, flows to the architect, and then finds its solution through a series of clarifying discussions between the two. The design which results from that teacher-architect interaction will lead to a setting in which the child's learning will more likely be optimized both in efficiency and in richness. The resultant setting should be so obviously functional that teachers, children, their parents, and all others whose dollars support the schools will feel that the time and resources which went into the project were well spent.

SPECIFICATIONS FOR EDUCATIONAL PROGRAMS

What should be included in a design to provide optimum education for mentally retarded pupils? For blind pupils? For pupils with behavioral disorders?

How does one begin to set down the elements essential to sound and productive schooling for deaf pupils? For speech handicapped pupils? For crippled pupils?

The first step toward the answer to each of those questions calls for an identification of the educational objectives which local special education experts agree upon for handicapped children. The second step is to specify the facilities and procedures and material which are essential for the accomplishments of the educational objectives. When linked together, the educational objectives and the facilities, the procedures and the materials needed to accomplish the objectives form *Educational Specifications*. They constitute the only solid base for designing schooling for the handicapped.

Educational Specifications can be general and they can be detailed. An example of a general specification could be that educable mentally retarded pupils will have occupational-vocational-technical instruction between the ages of fifteen and eighteen. That *general* specification does give an important clue as to what should be planned. However, it is even more useful to know details. For instance, it would be of significance to know that the initial teaching would be done in the school rather than out on the job; that the occupations would include assembly, wrapping and packaging, delivery, cafeteria operations, and stock room helping and maintenance; that simulation will be one of the main procedures used plus actual work experience in the school; and that the materials will, for the most part, be supplies used by teachers and by the food services and maintenance divisions of the schools. From such examples, it is evident that these specifics, if known by the architect, can contribute to more appropriate design of the school environment.

PLAN REGULAR SCHOOLS FOR HANDICAPPED PUPILS

It is no longer appropriate to include a half-page description of a *special education classroom* and allow that to suffice. It is true that the handicapped pupil, his parents, and his teachers did at one time accept the castoff and the leftover, whatever couldn't be used by the regular classes. But that day is past. Now exceptional children are more and more *a part of* education rather than *apart from* it.

It would be well for all architects and educators to plan all kinds of regular schools as though all kinds of handicapped pupils will attend them. Also, it would be well for all educators and architects to plan all kinds of special schools so they could readily be used by nonhandicapped pupils. This allows for *reverse inclusion,* a term developed in the public schools of Tacoma. It is illustrated by bringing nonhandicapped children from the regular elementary school into the school wing designed for educating deaf pupils. The nonhandicapped pupils mingle with the latter in various social and teaching situations. It also allows the space to be used by regular classes if it is no longer needed for special education.

More and more, nursery-kindergarten, elementary, middle, junior high, and senior high schools have handicapped pupils scattered through them and receiving some special education. That comes about because of two operating principles regarding special education. One is decentralization, which spreads special education facilities and resources to all neighborhood schools, and makes it possible to mount high quality special education services in any school with few exceptions. The second principle, mentioned earlier, is mainstreaming or inclusion or integration, which locates handicapped children as they begin school, monitors them in kindergarten and first grade, and continues them in regular classes, while providing resources in manpower and instruction to help the regular class teacher give the handicapped pupils the help they need.

WHAT IS INCLUDED IN *CURRICULUM*

Teachers use the term *curriculum* to "encompass the instructional activities planned and provided for pupils by the school or school system. The curriculum, therefore, is the planned interaction of pupils with instructional content, instructional resources, and instructional processes for the attainment of educational objectives." [122] Thus, the curriculum is the knowledge and ideas and skills important to pupils, as well as the books, tapes, films, maps, and other things used by teacher and pupils; curriculum is even considered by some to include, as well, the processes, methods, and techniques used in teaching.

When we call for schools in general which have the capability to accommodate exceptional children, we speak of that capability in more than the sense of physical accommodation. We mean it in the sense of *curriculum* as well.

PUTTING THE *CURRICULUM* INTO OPERATIONAL TERMS

The next two portions of this section deal first with the curricular area which can be called the world of work, and second, with the curricular area we call play. They will exemplify the intimate connections between what is taught, to whom it is taught, and where and how it is taught.

The early portion of the section which follows gives some ideas about readying exceptional children to make places for themselves in the productive economic life of the community. The discussion is presented as an example of the kind of consideration which needs to be given to *all* aspects of the curriculum, not only that which has a vocational orientation. Also, it is well known that social skills and manual skills are equally important in the great majority of work settings, so we emphasize them both. Furthermore, we emphasize the recent revival of the belief that effective and rewarding life experience in the world of work must be rooted in learning in the earliest years and cultivated in the middle school and high school.

As has been said, many educators interpret curriculum as all of a child's learning experiences which take place in a school. If we put together the instruction by teachers, the setting in which learning takes place, and the instruction related activities of the entire school staff, we find that these are what make up the curriculum. It is the curriculum, chiefly, which the educator must describe to the architect in the form of the Education Program. That Education Program (whose development is detailed in the next chapter) is the basic reference from which the architect creates the design of the learning environment.

If there are to be new elements injected into the curriculum in any new structure, it is very important to note that to the architect. Also, if at all possible, those new elements should be tried out by teachers in the present setting or in a simulation of the new setting. Such tryouts and appraisals of their results can save many potentially expensive or wasteful errors in designing the new facility.

PREPARATION FOR THE WORLD OF WORK

There are some who may take the position that the elementary and secondary education of handicapped children should not be concerned with vocational evaluation or any emphasis whatsoever on the preparation of employable skills. Others will feel as strongly that education is preparation for a full independent life, and this is not possible for either the normal or handicapped adult without the development of employable skills.

Interests, experiences, and intelligence will often guide the normal child and young adult to employment opportunities and ultimately to the selection of a career. Modern elementary, middle, and high schools include career and work concepts deliberately. Guidance counselors are available and helpful particularly if the student chooses to continue education beyond the secondary level. The experiences and advice of the family will be helpful and meaningful. The pattern of educational opportunity and development for normal children is established, and the quality of education in America testifies to the validity and success of our effort.

But can we say the same for the educational program derived for the handicapped, which is usually characterized by modification of what is considered good educational preparation for normal children and often with little or no emphasis on vocational evaluation at an early age? Many pay lip service to solving the problem of employing the handicapped. However, a creative analytical effort is needed to devise an educational program that will satisfy the real needs of the handicapped and particularly their most important need, and the only one that can insure independence, namely, productive employment.

We must rethink this aspect of the education of the handicapped. In doing so, we must rethink the provision of physical space for vocational preparation of the handicapped.

A recent sample survey indicates that not more than 10 percent of physically handicapped adults are employed at a level of income that allows financial independence. Among the educable mentally retarded the percentage is substantially higher, but the proportion could still be increased.

Society has a choice to make. Our educational system can prepare the handicapped by developing initial skills that can lead to employment opportunities. We can also continue to merely modify the accepted regular program by accepting lifelong support of the handicapped in residential institutions or by providing a degree of independence through welfare programs. Both methods are costly. And both ignore society's obligation to the handicapped to give them the same opportunities for a creative independent life that we offer to all who are normal.

In any discussion of employment opportunity preparation, the first tendency will be to categorize opportunity on the basis of handicap; opportunities for the blind, opportunities suited to intelligent cerebral palsied, or opportunities for educable retarded. If the categories could be clearly defined and consistent, solutions could be devised for each. But they are not. We must accept and be concerned with a whole range of handicaps that vary in degree of intensity and frequently occur in multiples.

Normal children have so many opportunities to develop social and manual skills that little importance is attached to them in establishing the objectives of an educational program. This, however, is not true for the majority of handicapped children, particularly those with physical and mental deficits. While they may have the same opportunities to develop manual skills, they usually fall far behind their peers because of the lack of strength, the absence of complete motor control, and limited mobility. The same is true for social skills.

If the objective of the educational program is to prepare the handicapped child to cope with the normal world about him, more than the usual emphasis must be placed on his development of manual skills and social skills. He must develop them to improve his ability in self-care, his performance in home care, and, of greatest importance, his ultimate employment in productive work, and therefore his independence as an individual. In most instances, we may be certain that his employment opportunities will be limited. While some young adults may follow normal channels of education and employment, the majority, of necessity, will have to develop social and manual skills to the maximum of their capabilities in order to reach any degree of self-sufficiency. Consequently, if an objective of the educational program is to improve all of the child's skills to the maximum, the development of his social and manual skills may be equal in importance to the three R's.

While vocational training and future employment may be the ultimate goal, the development of social and manual skills at the elementary level is in a grey area. The occupational therapist and the physical education teacher are the most concerned about manual skills, but many schools do not have adaptive physical education or an occupational therapist. If they do, they will often be part-time. The general physical education teacher will be concerned, but manual dexterity can be but a small part of that teacher's effort which is directed toward the total physical development of the child. The art teacher will be concerned, but interest in manual dexterity is usually overshadowed by efforts to stimulate creative activity. Whether the child can color precisely to the edge of a line may not be considered important by the art teacher and may even be ignored in favor of more creative activity if the importance of manual dexterity as preparation for future employment is not appreciated.

If the above is correct, should we reexamine the objectives of the instructional program to determine whether the development of an essential skill should be fractured into a group of classes where the skill itself is considered secondary? Or should there be a separate area of instruction devoted primarily to the improvement of both gross and fine motor functions, and motor coordination with emphasis on manual dexterity and eye-hand coordination, all in preparation for the ultimate development of work habits and skills through the manipulation of real tools and equipment?

It is not our purpose here to say what *should* be done so far as developing social and manual skills are concerned. Rather, it is an attempt to stimulate the design team, teacher, architect, parents, administrators, and others, to think through what they really want by way of curriculum and how they will accomplish it. Then the design can truly reflect the functions to be performed.

Each child will learn from what he does, and the content of his school experiences can be varied within the limits of the educational objectives. The examples his teacher may use may be abstract or realistic, probably both. If, however, the teacher is mindful of preparation for the world of work, examples can be selected that will reinforce his development of employable skills rather than only parallel them. Likewise, physical space and equipment can further strengthen this effort. The development of his academic skills can be applied to real life experience, reinforcing both. While he is learning to read, he will certainly read books; but he can also learn to read signs, particularly cautionary signs. While he is learning numbers, he can also learn to read clocks and dials. As he advances toward graduation, he can learn to read and fill out job application forms and participate in a work-study program.

Many new schools have provided a small store for the multiple purposes of learning to shop, learning to count by handling items of merchandise, learning to make simple calculations by handling money, and learning to operate equipment with a simple cash register or adding machine. To elaborate further, the store experience can be used to apply other work related skills: to arrange in order, to sort by color or shape or size, to wrap with paper and seal with tape or knotted string, or to stock a shelf. A bulletin board with removable letters will provide experience in sorting by alphabet or numbers. An intercom phone can teach how to use the instrument, how to respond, how to dial, and how to record a message. Bulk dry materials and a scale can supplement their experience in the use of measures. Handmade signs can call attention to *sale* items. When handicapped children reach the secondary level, they should have many opportunities to test their manipulative skills and their interests in as many areas as the school staff and equipment will permit. Some will already have decided to go to higher education, but others will have to begin analyzing their skills, finding their interests, and initiating a program that will develop their skills to the maximum of their physical and intellectual abilities. They may naturally gravitate to certain areas of work or may require the guidance of a vocational counselor. In some of the Scandinavian countries, their preparation for work is directed not only to a general area but to a specific job for which the knowledge and skill can be precisely defined.

Many books, brochures, and other documents are available to guide a designer to an acceptable solution of the problem of planning a shop area. Consequently, rather than duplicate this material, we will confine our comments to the specific problems of providing vocational skill areas for the handicapped. These may be in individual self-contained areas, particularly when dirt and dust are generated, or in an open space area.

Shop Areas

The precautions of safety and protection from hazards which are usually provided for normal children should, of course, also be provided for handicapped children. But that is not enough. There should be emergency power shutoff locations within a few steps of any point where the teacher may be. To accommodate wheelchairs, the aisles between pieces of equipment must be wider with the result that the shop area may be larger. As it increases in physical size, the problem of complete visual control becomes more imperative.

Equipment may be installed to provide for work experiences in metal, wood, or plastics, and will usually include equipment to drill, grind, and buff. Since some of the children may be more susceptible to bronchial illness, particular attention must be given to dust collection and removal. Ideally, the area will be ventilated to provide six to ten air changes an hour, and, if the air is recirculated, it should be filtered before returning to the normal ventilation system.

Experience has shown that welding is a skill that can serve the handicapped, particularly the educable mentally retarded. Training in elementary welding will require a fume hood with positive exhaust and, of course, a welding bench resistant to high temperatures.

If spray painting is to be done on wood or metal, it is probable that the building code will require a specially ventilated spray booth.

At some point in the shop complex, drafting tables and equipment should be available for elementary instruction in the description of three dimensional form on two dimensional paper. When provided, the drafting table should be designed to permit a student in a wheelchair to use it.

Wood working equipment, the usual hand tools, benches, and vise will normally be provided to allow the development of skill required to work the material. In addition to this, however, floor space and work benches should be provided for experience in refinishing or reupholstering existing used furniture.

An area for instruction in the maintenance and repair of small engine equipment should be considered. The servicing of small motorized power equipment is increasing as the number of power lawn mowers, home snow removal and small tractors in use increases. Blade sharpening is a related skill.

One school stimulated interest in the development of mechanical skills by encouraging shopkeepers and others in the community to contribute equipment that might be repaired: record players, adding machines, radios, clocks, anything that a young adult might wish to own. Any student could earn one by repairing it!

House Care

While it is true that children and young adults could be taught the care of their homes while at their own homes, professional instructions will improve the development of their skills and their performance. Given wall surfaces of different materials, they can learn to wash paint or ceramic tile, clean wallpaper, and care for wood paneling. They can be taught to wash and care for floors of wood, ceramic tile, resilient tile, and carpet. A built-in double hung window will serve for instruction in window washing and care and operation of shades, curtains, and venetian blinds.

A working bath room will provide opportunities to care for a toilet, a sink, a tub, a shower curtain, a medicine cabinet, and a mirror, and to replace toilet paper rolls and refill kleenex dispensers.

A domestic size kitchen will allow instruction in the care and use of a range, refrigerator, dishwasher, mixer, hood, compartment sink, and utensils, dishes and flatware. If space is available, an adjoining alcove can house a laundry tray, washer, dryer, clothes line, and possibly a small ironer. A cooperative effort with a commercial laundry can develop job opportunities.

Food Service

In addition to the domestic kitchen, it would be well to consider a food preparation and food service area for the many who can develop employable skills. If the school prepares its own lunches in its own kitchen, instruction and practice could be given to selected young adults. Those with the potential can develop the skill of a short order cook or cook's helper, in learning to grille and deep fry as well as serving and wrapping take out orders. A table and a restaurant booth with menus, napkins, flatware, glasses, sugar dispensers, salt and pepper shakers, and bottled condiments will allow waitress or bus boy practice. Order taking and serving experience will generate confidence.

Preparation of skills for employment in a commercial bakery will best be done in a cooperative effort with an existing company, preferably nearby. These skills can include material selecting, mixing, rolling, baking, decorating and packaging.

Nursing Service and Aides

With the increase in the senior citizen population, there are increased job opportunities in the care of the invalided, infirm, or the elderly. Instructions can be initiated with typical hospital equipment: a hospital bed, an over bed table, bedpan, wheelchair, linen, and a hospital doll.

Sewing

The normal home economics classroom may provide opportunities for instructions in sewing, but children without complete motor control may have difficulty with the normal speed of sewing machines. To serve this group, there are sewing machines available with gear shift control allowing the machine to operate very slowly but with full power. The speed can be increased as the student's skill improves. The work table and cutting table for sewing instruction should be at a height convenient to a young adult in a wheelchair. Reachable storage cupboards and a hanging rod are also essential.

Landscape Maintenance

If the budget of a school will permit, employable skills may be developed for greenhouse work. Students can learn to fertilize, plant, pot, bud, prune, and transplant. All outdoors is available for teaching ground care, mowing, edging, trimming, weeding, raking, and trash disposing.

Other Off Campus Work Stations

There are many areas of opportunity for the employment of the handicapped that require the development of skills not easily taught in the school environment. In many instances, the school can introduce the student to the work, but the development of the skill is best accomplished by on-the-job training. The commercial laundry and commercial bakery have already been mentioned. A career as a private or public telephone operator is possible for many. Printing and duplicating companies offer opportunities. Photography and related processes of reproduction should be explored. Piano tuning has long been open to the blind. Skills in these areas can be developed easily if the school is willing to develop a special program for *learners,* a program in which the students spend time in school and on the job as the convenience of their handicap may indicate. In any event, on-the-job training is desirable whenever it is possible.

Ideally, students would develop employable skills in school and exercise these skills under the supervision of their teacher until they were ready to perform independently. If the skill was one that could be utilized by the school, (serving in the cafeteria line) the student would progress to school work-experience and finally to community work-experience with employment by others.

Union-Government Cooperation

One of the principal problems of employment of the handicapped has not been solved in this country, but successful employment practices operate in the Netherlands. Our industry, like theirs, is unionized. Union membership, regulations, and wage scales are generally based on the full-time performance of their members. To our knowledge, there is no provision for a shorter working day for those who do not have the work tolerance to perform for eight consecutive hours, five days a week. Some handicapped persons may be able to work only a part day. Others may be able to work an 8-hour day provided that they have more generous rest periods than normal. This is a stumbling block to the employment of the handicapped that must be solved and can easily be solved as the Netherlands has recognized. There, a handicapped person is welcome in any union in which he can perform the required work. He is paid union wages for his work. If his working hours are limited to less than a full working day or if his production is below normal because of motor-perceptual or other deficits, his employer pays him full compensation for a full work week at regular union wages. His employer and the government then evaluate his performance and assign a value to his service. If this is less than the employer paid him, the government reimburses the employer for the difference between work paid for and work performed. The cost to taxpayers is considerably less than the cost of total support of the handicapped person as a part of the welfare program.

Handicapped individuals are not unusual in their normal concern about new experiences and their tendency to cling to the familiar. Some of the Scandinavian schools for the handicapped have recognized the fear and uncertainty of a young adult leaving the school and preparing to accept employment in a somewhat unfamiliar world and probably away from home. Some have provided an apartment for house parents and students within the school building in order to prepare for this adjustment. The students live as they would sharing an apartment in the working world, shopping for food and service, helping prepare the food, doing housekeeping, providing their own amusements and recreation, and learning to use their leisure time. When they graduate, employed and established in a manner of living, they do so with confidence. Some countries have helped by building transitional hostels and permanent apartment homes designed specifically to serve the handicapped.

ROLE OF PLAY IN THE EDUCATION OF HANDICAPPED PUPILS

What we said about *work* in the preceding section applies to *play* and similarly affects all human beings, young or old, handicapped or not. But it has particular application to special education.

Play as a Basic Learning Experience

Play can be a child's most effective learning experience. For the baby, it is often the first learning experience in self-generated initiative, curiosity, and imagination. He responds to color, to movement, and to sound at an accelerating rate and with increasingly joyful exuberance. He reaches for a toy and learns that things roll, turn, rattle, and squeak. Soon he learns that he can manipulate objects to do what he wants them to do. Play is the essence of the normal child's world, but in many instances, *the handicapped child must be taught to play.*

Most teachers believe that the child's intellectual, emotional, and physical development, even within limited capacities, should develop simultaneously, and they accept the challenge of teaching the child to play in a manner that will encourage his maximum development.

As has been said before, the handicapped child learns from what he does, and only from what he does. If his physical deficit reduces the number of learning experiences, it is our obligation to enrich these experiences. Play is the essence of his world. It provides his first learning experiences, and these should be rich, varied, and meaningful. It is true that play amuses. It can also be the critical learning experience that can minimize his deficit if the teacher guides his experiences with imagination, inventiveness, and skill.

We must use the pupil's play experience to enhance visual motor coordination and spatial relationship development as well as physical development. Play may be carefully structured physical education, or it may be free play. Both are essential, but free play is more appropriate after school hours. Structured play which combines play with affective experiences, with cognitive challenge, and with motor and manual dexterity is the essence of the teacher's problem. Play experience should be meaningful, with clear objectives and thoughtful guidance.

Handicapped Children Need to be Taught to Play

Group play may not come naturally to many handicapped children. Until they come to school they may not have had a chance to play with other children or to play on play equipment.

It is simple to amuse a child on a piece of moving equipment. It may be exhilarating and exciting, but generally speaking, it is not teaching. Nor is it learning.

It is more difficult to devise a learning experience in which the child, not the equipment, does the moving in self-improvised, self-initiated play, and is encouraged by an imaginative, inventive teacher. Success, not just amusement, must be the result of the play experience. Just as a blind child must have continuous success in play experiences by negotiating and manipulating the unseen in order to develop his sense of independence and security, the sighted but otherwise handicapped child must succeed, too. And the challenge for the teacher is to guide them both to successful play experiences which have definable intellectual, social, and physical objectives and outcomes.

The child's play world must be safe and secure and able to attract children into lengthy games of imagination. It is not enough to provide equipment for athletic feats and competitive exercises. The child's recreational environment should provide him with a variety of activities filled with opportunities for fantasy, role playing, and acting out.

The goal is to enhance coordination and auditory, visual, and motor perceptual faculties; and to reduce the deficits in background through role playing and provision of actual experiences where real life experiences have been limited. If sense perceptions are faulty, children can have difficulty in coordinating physical movement. Play can develop mobility and dexterity.

Too often the physical education of the handicapped child has been characterized by mere modifications of what is considered good for normal children (i.e. competitive games in a basketball court gymnasium!). If play is to be a learning experience, it must be guided participation in self-improvised and self-initiated game play. This learning objective is not usually possible on the conventional equipment common to many playgrounds where the child rides on slides, swings, seesaws, or whirling platforms. Here the child gets limited exercise of motor or perceptual skills, because the equipment, rather than the child, does the moving. Educational play equipment should have the characteristic of tantalizing the exceptional child into a fanstasy world where he can fly to the moon, dive under the sea, play follow the leader to the top of the mountain, and drive the train around the curve! It must be an experience that engages the whole child, body, mind, and emotions. Then and only then can the youngster profit and learn from the experience in an optimum way.

A playground for blind children has special problems because the youngsters must first be taught to use the equipment. If it is to serve its purpose, it must be equipment they can use, not just ride on. For the most part, it should be climbing equipment with the various different characteristics of numerous hand holds, foot holds, struts, bars, and links within easy reach of legs and arms. It can have a perch to climb to and grips to hold onto around the top. Blind pupils must learn to see by touch, by sound, and by smell. Herbs and other plants provide stimulating odors and textures. The opportunity to play must be provided in a manner that will guarantee success in negotiating the unseen. To do so is essential in gaining a sense of independence and security.

The playground and its equipment should have spatial variety. It should have high places and low places, big and little places, dark places, light places, open places and narrow places! There should be things to go over, go under, go through, around, into and out of. There should be a fence to look over and another to look under. When designing the play area, it should be remembered that equipment should be close together or compact enough that children stimulate one another and together move easily from one piece to another.

Safety, of course, is imperative. Beware of movable equipment that is completely beyond the mastery of a poorly coordinated child. While all equipment should be challenging and stimulating, it must also be safe and secure and eliminate the child's fear of being hurt. If the play area is not fenced, it can be surrounded by benches to help orient the children.

Generally, the play area will have different kinds of surfaces: hard tops for paths, walks and areas for wheeled equipment, a grass area for exploration, slopes, a hill for sliding, hollows, trees and shrubs, a pit for jumping into, and a garden area with water, sand and clay for digging, and maybe even a cave! A fish pond, bird bath, bird feeder and bird house on a pole, and a tree house can be placed in the garden area. One school has animals running freely within a fenced play area.

There is a variety of equipment available today: portable sand boxes and wading pools, a portable water play tub on casters, shallow pools, and huge rubber mattresses for falling and rolling.

Play Space Treatment in Other Countries

One of the most unusual playgrounds is at Geelsgard in Denmark. This residential school for physically handicapped children has provided a *building yard* almost an acre in extent that is covered with raw and painted structures built by the children under minimal supervision. Some are houses for pets, some are hideaways for children, some are for climbing and some are for sitting under. To the adult there appears to be no rhyme or reason to the assembly, but the result is a tantalizing assortment of spaces for imaginative play. Built from scrap lumber, the cost was remarkably little.

In New Zealand, there are parent constructed play areas adjacent to schools. The play space, like the one in Denmark, makes use of materials like logs washed up from the sea, large natural stones, and heavy marine mooring ropes.

The Effect of Climate

In colder climates, play areas should be sheltered from wind; in warm climates, part of the play area should be roofed to provide shade. Many children sunburn easily, and mongoloid children are particularly prone to respiratory illness, so care must be exercised not to create a wind tunnel rather than a covered porch.

Consideration for Children on Wheelchairs or Crutches

Part of each play area should be a teaching-learning area if physically handicapped children on crutches and wheelchairs are in attendance. They will need instruction and practice in walking or riding on different surfaces; bricks, concrete, wood, sand, grass, gravel. They will need a place to practice going up or down a curb, crossing a street between stop lights and, if possible, practice getting on and off streetcars and buses by the use of a stationary model. If this is not possible, instruction at the carbarn or bus garage can be a satisfactory substitute under some circumstances.

Aquatic Play

When the budget has permitted, schools for handicapped children have provided swimming pools, generally indoor for year round use. These may be of three different types depending on the teaching objectives.

If the primary purpose is therapy, the pool will have a level floor with water approximately three feet deep at a temperature of approximately 90 degrees. This will normally be under the direction of the physical therapist and is not generally considered for swimming instruction or recreation, but could be often so used for hyperactive children because of the calming effect of the warm water. One pool of this type was used as a classroom by a speech therapist who had found that the hard tile surfaces gave excellent sound reinforcement. Yet the pool area was quiet. The warmth of the water and humidity made relaxed breathing easier for the children.

The more common pool is a normal pool for recreational water play and swimming. The water will not be as hot as the therapy pool. The design of such a pool is a technical problem which is well treated in *Swimming Pools—A Guide to Their Planning, Design, and Their Operation.*[72] Suffice to say here that it may be small or large but should have a deep end for diving. Often the shallow end of the pool is provided with steps or a ramp to make access easier for the physically handicapped and to preclude the use of a sling lift. Diving boards are common but if used by the blind must be carefully supervised.

The third and least common pool is a teaching pool whose only purpose is to teach swimming. It is generally smaller and has a stepped bottom to provide different depths from 30 inches to 5 feet. It is not a good recreational pool because of the hazard of the stepped bottom and because it cannot have a diving board.

CHAPTER X

THE PLANNING PROCESS

KEY ELEMENTS IN SCHOOL PLANT PLANNING

"If general education is remiss in bringing to architectural programming the best in research designing, special education for handicapped children is typified by an even less scientific approach."[44]

WE COULD NOT AGREE MORE with the above statement. Our own observations parallel those of Cruickshank and Quay who support the need for more orderly, systematic, and planned approaches in the development of special education facilities. In commenting on the current state of affairs, individuals working on the Architecture and Special Education Project[2] said:

> Visits to recently constructed buildings showed lack of local planning. The visits also indicated many educational or architectural decisions based on educated hunches of architect and educator rather than on definitive research and planning primarily on the part of business or administration type educators. Billions of dollars in school construction are being invested by the nation through local boards of education with practically no research data reflecting the known interface between environmental design and the needs of the learner and the learning situation.[44]

An orderly planning process, if followed, will help to maximize the impact of research findings and tested experience on future structures. There is only a little definitive research applicable to the interface of the teaching act and the space in which it occurs, but what there is should be used. As far as planning is concerned, however, there are well-worked-out procedures available. Their use can reduce the incidence of impulsive decisions or narrow gauge approaches to the serious problems of designing schools and schooling for handicapped pupils.

[158]

STEPS IN PLANNING

This overview delineates the main elements to be considered when getting ready to construct or remodel a school facility. The following items give a bare introduction to what must be done; each item needs to be elaborated in relation to designing for the education of exceptional children and youth.

One use of the overview is to give a brief picture of the total process to be dealt with. Perhaps the list of key elements will also be useful as a check list. The educator and the architect responsible might well periodically review the items in the overview to see that all have been accounted for.

Harold W. Boles[33] gives a list (see below) of eleven sequential steps he considers essential. He shows them as follows, reading from the bottom up.

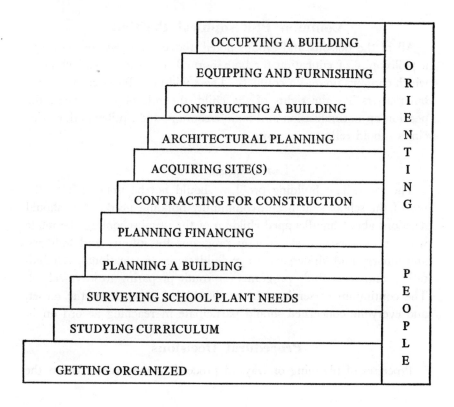

Boles' figure implies that there is a preferred sequence to the jobs which need to be done. The figure also implies that the first step is a foundation for the second; the first and second are foundations for the third; and so on. And the vertical column on the right indicates the crucial need for continuing communication with persons who need to be kept aware of what is going on and what is projected.

For the *Getting Organized* step, the responsible special educators will need to attend to at least ten elements. These are, in some cases, adaptations and extensions of points made by Boles.

Evidence of Need

The board of education, the community, the superintendent, and the regional and state educational officials must have data in readily understandable form which demonstrates unequivocally that the need exists and there must be agreement on the part of all as to the need.

Common Philosophical Position

All of the persons and groups noted above must pay allegiance to a philosophy of education for both normal and exceptional children which contains no major conflicts. There will be differences, of course, but matters like the rights of the child, the role of the teacher, the position on normalization and mainstreaming, and similar major principles should reflect concensus.

Long-Range View

The immediate building problem should not be isolated from the rest of the school system and community building needs. Nor should decisions about handicapped children of the usual school age be made without reference to stimulation programs for infants and toddlers, and nursery and kindergarten age children, or to vocational, rehabilitation, and work-study programs for youth preparing to leave school. The continuum of services theme should be struck from the outset, and everyone concerned should participate in reaching accord on it.

Procedural Decisions

Processes of planning or ways of proceeding may vary. When the method is determined, it should be stated and agreed upon among the superintendent, the board of education, the parent groups, the chief special educators, and the others who have responsibility. Once adopted, procedural guidelines should be changed only with the informed consent of all concerned.

Professional and Technical Terms

Special educators, regular educators, administrators, architects and other professional planners, community agencies, members of the health professions, and others involved will have to make conscious efforts to learn each other's special languages, at least to the extent that a base is established for common communications.

Legal and Volunteer Agency Liaison

School construction calls for approvals for compliance with laws and regulations from many agencies at the state, regional, and local levels, and they vary from state to state. Designing space to accommodate persons with handicaps often adds complications for those approvals and sometimes means the involvement of agencies other than the usual ones. That is made even more complex by the large numbers of volunteer agencies who work with exceptional children and youth and represent parental points of view in an organized way. A careful enumeration of the legal and volunteer agencies and a check on what needs to be done in connection with each of them, is a fundamentally important part of getting organized.

Table of Organization of Participants

Referring to the steps in Boles' table, a list of names, addresses, titles, and roles should be made. Once drawn up, that list can be divided into those who get copies of all correspondence or only certain memos. Formal approval of the list by the board of education, the superintendent, and the chief responsible special educator is very desirable. It should, of course, be possible to add others to the list as the work progresses if that is advisable. Everyone on the list should know who everyone else is too.

Responsibility and Authority

The board of education or whatever body has legal authority should assign specific elements of work in keeping with recommendations of the superintendent or other chief executive officers. The assignments should be clear, with any necessary overlaps noted and recognized. The principal should obtain that *authority should be commensurate with responsibility.* Also, the lines of reporting should be expilicated in detail with due attention by the board to the recommendations of its head administrative officers in that regard.

Sequence of Events

The sequence of events for the entire project would not be worked out in full detail in the *getting organized* stage. It would be advisable, however, to formally adopt a system for laying out those details at this stage. We recommend Program Evaluation and Review Technique (PERT),[41] though there are many other systems which could be employed to essentially the same end.

Deadlines and Expectations

It can be costly to delay construction and it can be costly to move too swiftly into construction. One of the advantages of PERT is that it contains a mechanism which helps planners come to rational decisions about how to use and how to estimate the need for time on any project or subcomponent of the project. Once it is determined, all parties involved should be aware of the time estimates, time constraints, and the kinds of occurrences which can alter the time schedule loading from *getting organized* to *occupying a building.*

EDUCATIONAL PLANNING

Teachers are no strangers to planning. Their educational work is largely divided among planning, organizing materials and space, conducting instruction, assessing the results, and carrying through the cycle again.

But planning time is something that has been difficult for the teacher to obtain. Whatever the reasons, time to plan has been limited in the teacher's day. It is rare, now, that teachers have more than

15 percent of their day available for planning and related aspects of preparation for teaching. More is needed.

Except for an occasional *lucky hit,* an unplanned or too quickly planned lesson lands in the range between poor and disastrous. The same is true of school building and facilities. Without sufficient opportunity for careful and thorough planning, the most likely results are dissatisfaction and waste.

TEACHER INVOLVEMENT IN PLANNING

Teacher opinion and judgment is a very important part of the realistic base from which architectural planning should proceed. Speaking generally, teachers feel they are less involved in school policy decisions than they should be. Also, there is an increased desire on the part of teachers to be consulted on school policy matters.

In 1968 and 1972, a nationwide sample of teachers responded to queries about how much they had participated in discussions leading to determinations about the items listed below.[124]

Topics	Not As Involved As I Wanted To Be	
	1968 (percent)	1972 (percent)
Curriculum Decisions	37.3	43.3
Selection of Text Books	34.0	35.4
Determination of Teacher Salaries	39.2	47.2
Determining and Implementing Grievance Procedures	21.9	32.0
Determination of Fringe Benefits	36.3	42.6
Procedures for Selecting School Principal	31.3	51.9
Adherence to Code of Ethics	22.9	32.1
Establishing School Calendar	35.2	44.8
Procedure for Teacher Evaluation	35.1	47.4
Student Discipline Procedures	31.9	43.1

Three of the most highly rated items in which teachers desired more involvement are also three items of major importance in planning the design of a school facility. They are curriculum decisions, the school calendar, and the selection of its principal. The importance of the first, the curriculum, is quite direct and obvious. The other two are more subtle, though no less significant. For example, the adoption of a year round school calendar can have a dramatic influence on school design. As far as the selection of the principal is concerned, the criteria used in picking that person are profoundly important in their potential effect on the character of the school, however indirect that influence might be.

This is not to minimize the importance of the other teacher concerns listed above. All are significant. Rather, the point is to emphasize the fact that teachers feel they have valuable input, that they want their ideas to be included in the policy making matrix, and that the architects and educators responsible for planning need to have direct and ready access to teacher viewpoints all along the way. It should be noted, too, that for each of the ten items, the four years from 1968 to 1972 produced more teachers who said they were not as involved in decisions as they wanted to be. Thus, there is good reason to expect real cooperation from individual teachers and teacher groups because of their evident motivation toward wanting to be involved.

PLANNING FOR INSTRUCTIONAL MATERIALS

Because of the constant development of new instructional materials and improved instructional procedures, it is not feasible to be absolutely specific about some of the space needs which relate to instruction. One appropriate way to deal with that problem is to share as much information as possible with the architect in the following manner.

Make two lists in parallel. On the left, include what the instructional space requirements would be if you were moving into the space *today* and could have what you consider the best available instructional materials and staffing. Then, in the parallel column on the right, indicate what the requirements would be if the significantly different instructional approaches you know are on the horizon were to materialize. This latter should not be an exercise in daydreaming. It should make use of the knowledge and judgment of special education teachers and staff members from instructional materials centers. The lists might look like this:

Instructional Materials Space Needs in New Facility
for Immediate Pupil and Teacher Access

Current	*Future*
Printed catalogue of local school Resources Center materials.	Microfilm viewer of materials in local school Resources Center (Replacement of current catalogue).
Pupil desk-chair combination with built-in projector for programmed exercises.	Videotape projector linked to distant bank of programmed instruction exercises available to pupil or teacher by dial or phone verbal call up. (In addition to current pupil desk-chair).
Headquarters area for teacher aide in proximity to instructional materials storage area of (size).	Headquarters area for two teacher aides and two peer teaching assistants (part-time, high school students giving one hour every two days), and materials storage area 50% more than current size.
etc.	*etc.*

Each of the preceding, of course, might be accompanied by actual dimensions of currently used space or currently needed space. Photos and pictures are of value, also. The central idea is to specify the actual uses and the actual materials to all possible extent so that all members of the design team, educators, architects and others have the same facts to consider as they work.

VISITING AN ESTABLISHED SCHOOL TO GLEAN IDEAS

There are many good reasons for architects, board of education members, teachers, school administrators, and community representatives to visit existing schools during the planning process. In order to get the most out of such visits, the following suggestions are relevant:

1. Have your own educational program document completed and studied by everyone involved before doing any visiting. This will allow those making the trip to look for ideas about the

form of the new facility in relation to decisions already made about the specific functions the new facility is to perform.

2. Be sure that the trip has real promise of being helpful before spending substantial amounts of time and money on it. That can be done by

   a. Detailed correspondence and telephone conversations with the director of special education and the principal of the school at the place under consideration for a visit. It is also good to have conversations or correspondence with one or more teachers in those communities.

   b. Obtain by mail and study copies of the educational program document that was used in designing the building, pictures of the plant, and related drawings and specifications.

   c. Determine if there are similar schools in the same region, visits to which might be included in the same trip.

3. Always send a team on the visit, never just one person. Three or four persons is the best group size and should represent teachers, experts in educational planning, board and community members, administration, and the architectural firm.

4. Take plenty of time to look and talk. One more day on a visit is a small investment when compared to the possible cost of making errors in such an enterprise. Interview parents, pupils, and especially teachers, the school support staff, custodians, and principals. Let them tell you about the problems in the school as well as its assets. If possible, locate the planners of the facility and ask them about the fit between what was planned and the reality of the present operation.

5. Be sure that every person on the team has an assignment as to what to examine and report. Each team should have a *captain* who has responsibility for coordinating the visitation activities.

6. Use tape recorders and still and movie cameras to record what you see and hear. These are small and portable enough to be easily manageable, and most schools have them available. Use them fully. The investment in cost is small in proportion to the amount and clarity of the information you can bring home to share with others.

7. Disseminate what you learn. Make it a matter of routine that every team which goes out to visit prepares a full report of its findings. That can include text and pictures. Distribute the report to all concerned people and make especially sure that it gets widespread distribution in the community and through the media.

By adapting the preceding seven points to local conditions, it is possible that visits to other schools can be made to greater advantage.

PLANNING OVER TIME

Generally, it takes about four years to move from the decision to develop a new school facility through construction to the occupancy of that facility. Use of planning aids such as PERT (Program Evaluation and Review Technique) can be helpful in spelling out the many activities which should go on during the stretch from ideas to actuality. There are many other planning procedures which could be used. But PERT has been adapted for educational purposes,[41] and thus, it will probably be a little more familiar to educators.

Using a planning system is essential to assure that proper time allotments are made for initial planning, meetings, visits, program writing, and other such significant activities leading up to decisions and actual construction. It is imperative that the planning system used is one that specifies which activities are to be accomplished, who is responsible, and at what time each event can be expected to be completed.

A schematic PERT Network [41] for the development of educational specifications is one way to meet the above requirement. Such a network is also of great importance in detailing the entire process of the work to be done beyond the preparation of the educational specifications. From that point on, however, the network development is primarily the task of the architect.

Architects are able, because of their professional training, to lay out planning processes of various types. Some of these can be adapted for educational program planning purposes. One scheme used frequently by architects is called a *decision train,* a layout showing decisions regarding time, space, and money. Those three are certainly among the key variables for any plan regarding building or remodeling.

CHAPTER XI

PREPARING THE EDUCATIONAL PROGRAM
PLANS FOR PLANNING

GIVEN TIME AND opportunity to participate as a team member in planning, how does a teacher, principal, supervisor, or other professional educator go about it? The way suggested here has no magic qualities. It does have two virtues; it is fairly simple and it has proven effective in the past.

Start with the following outline and move through it step by step:

1. Decide the general things you want to accomplish educationally and describe them in writing.

2. Sort the general things you want to do into broad educational categories.

3. Under each category write in greater detail the educational activities you envision, the reasons for them, and the results you hope to achieve with your pupils.

4. In all of the above three items, carefully avoid saying anything about the space or facilities you need to accomplish your objectives with your pupils.

5. Indicate in writing what your own approximate daily schedule will be to the best of your estimation. When it is not reasonable to give specific time periods, give approximate ranges.

6. Parallel the preceding step and show what you anticipate would be typical student schedules. Again, be as definite as is reasonable. However, it is better to be fairly general if that provides an accurate indication of reality.

7. Make two lists of equipment and materials. One list should contain everything which is *absolutely necessary* to sound and sufficient schooling for your pupils. The second list should contain everything which would be needed to raise the quality of education from adequate to excellent. (Teachers say that the

second list is usually shorter than the first list. Apparently, absolutely essential equipment and facilities need relatively little supplementing to significantly upgrade the potential quality level of instruction when teaching is initially competent.)

8. Alongside the items in the list made according to the preceding step, note whether or not it is necessary to have the equipment and materials for full-time use or whether occasional use is sufficient. For occasional use items, indicate the approximate times, each day or week, or any other special time consideration.

The above eight steps result in some of the most useful information for educational planning, when fitted to the rest of the educational specifications. The steps need some adaptations, of course, depending on the responsibilities of the professional person doing the planning. Sometimes, too, the steps can best be worked through by a group which shares responsibilities. But however they are applied, it is essential that some approach to planning for planning be adopted and used.

THE FUTURE OF MAINSTREAMING (INCLUSION)

There is reason to believe that exceptional children will more and more be educated in the elementary and secondary schools in the areas in which they reside. Only in very unusual cases will exceptional children be assigned to other schools or classes.

The most comprehensive study of special education costs to date [71] found the expense of transportation contributing in a major way to the high per pupil price for special education in certain categories of exceptionality. One of the five observations the study staff highlighted at the end of its report stated, ". . . it is recommended that, if at all possible, programs for exceptional children should be located in the same buildings, or at least on the same sites, where educational programs for regular children are housed."

Children classified as exceptional, as was pointed out earlier, include those who are blind, partially seeing, deaf, hard-of-hearing, brain injured, crippled and other health impaired, mentally retarded, mentally gifted, emotionally disturbed, socially maladjusted, educationally retarded, and those having learning disabilities and special learning problems. Separate special education schools or rooms will be supplied only to those of the above children whose conditions are so extreme as to make optimum education mostly in the regular class-room impossible, even with special help. It is anticipated that this will be a small proportion, mainly those with multiple handicaps.

The special educational help that is to be furnished to exceptional children in regular schools will be supplied by teacher-specialists assigned full-time or part-time to each building. Special education will usually be furnished in the regular class setting, in resource rooms, or in resource centers. Most exceptional children will be intermingled with all other children in homeroom groups. Each will have a schedule that includes as many regular classes of all kinds as possible. The schedule will be flexible enough to include, as needed, special instructional help from teacher-specialists at their resource rooms or centers. Children will be scheduled to a special education resource center whenever the special education teacher and the regular classroom teacher jointly determine the situation to warrant such action. That could be anywhere from one hour per week to as much as three or four hours per day.

For overall planning figures, it may be assumed that 15 percent of the enrollment, approximately 120 children in a school enrolling 800, will need some degree or kind of special education. The majority of those children, perhaps 50, will be classed as educable mentally retarded. They can be assumed to require, on the average, about half-time instruction in regular classes and half-time instruction in resource rooms, although there will be a considerable range of variation. The next largest number, perhaps 25, will need speech correction. They can be expected to be in regular classes at least 95 percent of the time and in the special education resource center the remainder of the time. The next largest group, perhaps 20, is the educationally retarded, or those with learning disabilities. They will average 15 percent of their time in the resource center and 85 percent in regular classes. Perhaps 10 of the children will be gifted and will use a resource teacher 10 percent of the time. The approximately 5 remaining exceptional children will represent a cross section of children with vision, hearing, crippling, adjustment, and other special learning problems. On the average, it may be assumed that they will use special education resource rooms or centers about 25 percent of the time and regular classrooms the remainder of the time.

The following will indicate what can be expected in curricular adjustments:

1. Physically handicapped: adapted physical education, mobility skills, and daily living skills.
2. Hearing handicapped: adapted language arts and music.
3. Visually handicapped: adapted reading, writing, mobility skills, and art.
4. Mentally gifted: curricular enrichment and acceleration.
5. Mentally retarded: curricular deceleration and vocational training.
6. Emotionally disturbed: restructured personal-social behavior; no special curricular emphases unless the pupil also has academic learning problems.
7. Speech handicapped: adapted speaking and listening aspects of language arts.
8. Educationally retarded (learning disabilities): no major or generalized curricular emphases; focus on correction of specific learning problems or deficits such as reading skills or arithmetic skills.

Building adaptations needed by exceptional children for mobility, access, and daily living uses have been pointed out in other sections. Educational specifications for the special education resource rooms or centers are also referred to elsewhere.

The objectives of education for exceptional children are closely similar to those of all other children. The special considerations have to do chiefly with the means of attaining the objectives and that is the reason teacher-specialists and resource rooms or centers are needed.

SPECIAL EDUCATION TRENDS RELATED TO SCHOOL DESIGN

The above paragraphs provide a thumbnail sketch of trends in special education today and in the recent past. The purpose of the short summary here is to bring the following points into focus.

1. Special education is tending to blend into and become an integral part of regular education.
2. Residential and special day schools are changing their roles to

provide more and more focus upon the highly complex educational special problems of children with multiple handicaps.

3. There is increased attention to systematic programs of encouragement and stimulation for very young handicapped children from infancy to five years with the aim of prevention or early correction of developmental deficits.

4. There are increasingly responsive relationships between special education and:

   a. Parents and volunteer groups expressing advocacy for handicapped children and youth's right to education.

   b. Related professional groups such as architects, vocational rehabilitation counselors, social workers, physicians and other members of the health professions, and legal and law enforcement personnel.

5. There will continue to be a need for buildings and other facilities designed to accommodate the handicapped. If anything, that need will be on the increase in the next decade.

THE PROGRAM

An education program is a document prepared to explain the nature of the educational activities conducted or to be conducted in a particular educational facility to any interested person who is not an educator. The program narrative is another term for the same document. It is usually prepared by an educator or a committee of educators to inform board of education members, architects, and others about all of the instructional and related procedures which need to be planned for in the design of a building.

The program outline which appears later in this section is for a public school which is to include special education for handicapped children. The education program outline was adapted from several existing outlines in order to make it illustrative.

At the outset, someone in the school system should be named to coordinate the writing of the educational program before detailed talks with the architect get started. The individual named should have enough knowledge about total school programs and enough authority and access to decision makers that the initial draft of the program writing moves with dispatch. Preferably, the education program document should be placed in the architect's hands in time for it to be studied thoroughly before design oriented discussions about the facility begin with the architect. (The terms *facility, building, structure,* and *school* are used as though they are synonymous in what follows.)

Probably no step is more important than that of reaching concensus on the education program. The first draft should be reviewed by the board of education, representative parent groups, teachers, administrators, community representatives, state department of education consultants, and any others who have legitimate interests, including students in certain instances. Finally, of course, decisions must be made by the administration and the board of education as to the content of the education program. That will be made easier in the long run by an open development process which involves all appropriate parties.

EDUCATION PROGRAM AND SPECIFICATIONS GUIDELINES

In a broad sense, the general nature of any school is determined by cultural, demographic, program, and site factors. Schools which include handicapped pupils will not be exceptions to that rule. There should be a great deal of opportunity for the prospective staff, the architect, and the planning coordinators to endow each school with a personality all its own, to be sure. However, certain overall design considerations which apply to all schools are now agreed upon and they are discussed in what follows.

The education program and specifications for a school contain the information necessary to allow an architect to design space which implements the program effectively and efficiently. In particular, the education program and specifications make clear the projected school's objectives, the size and nature of its student body, the staffing pattern, and the anticipated instructional, social and recreational activities. The specifications also include guidelines for what the children are to do and what they are to accomplish in the overall physical plant and in components of the plant such as general and specialized instructional areas. Equally important, the education program and specifications should transmit a feeling for the subjective qualities that the total atmosphere of the school is intended to convey.

The education program should be organized on the following outline or an adaptation which includes the same elements.

I. *THE SITUATION:* Describes the community and gives key demography.

II. *THE PROBLEMS:* States very briefly what educational problems will be solved by the new facility.

III. *SOLVING THE PROBLEMS:* A sequence of steps which are components of the educational program.

    A. *The Philosophy of the Teachers:* This states the principles which are basic to the educational program.

    B. *Legal and Regulatory Specifications:* This spells out any laws or regulations of the state and municipality which guide or limit school construction and which have bearing on this problem.

    C. *The Goals of Education Applicable to the School:* This section states goals which reflect accepted national, state, and local points of view regarding the functions and responsibilities of the schools. The goals stated here should be ones to which specific curricular objectives (which appear later in the education program) can relate.

    D. *Descriptions of the Learners to be Served by the School:* Here are listed the educationally relevant characteristics of the pupils who are expected to attend the school. The nature of the children can be explained under such headings as physical (i.e. varieties of learning styles and capabilities, rates of development); social (i.e. cultural and ethnic affiliations, background of social experience); interests (i.e. general and special); or under other headings which help to make clear the nature of the prospective pupils. The key purpose for preparing the descriptions, of course, is to assist in educational planning. Presumably, the architect and the educator can plan more effectively and harmoniously if they both realize that they are attempting to arrange, for certain kinds of children, the most efficient and effective physical space for teacher instruction and pupil learning.

E. *Staffing Pattern for the Facility:* This indicates the form the staff of the school will take and gives an indication of how responsibilities will be distributed. Since contemporary staffing is often diversified, it would be advisable first to show the absolute numbers of each kind of staff and second to explain their interactions. For the first, it might be useful to use such headings as:

1. *Full-Time Educational Professional Staff:* Indicate by title, certification, assignment, or any additional designation that will make clear, each person's professional competencies and expected responsibilities.

2. *Part-Time Professional Educational Staff:* Indicate by title, certification, assignment, or any additional designation that will make clear, each person's professional competencies and expected responsibilities.

3. *Full-Time Aides to Professional Staff:* Specify levels and extent of responsibilities. Use specific job titles to the extent possible.

4. *Part-Time Aides to Professional Staff:* Specify levels and extent of responsibilities. Use specific job titles to the extent possible.

5. *Adult Volunteers, Full-Time:* Describe sources of volunteers, backup organizations, if any, duties, and competencies.

6. *Adult Volunteers, Part-Time:* Describe sources of volunteers, backup organizations, if any, duties, and competencies.

7. *Student Teachers, Interns, and other Persons in Practicum Assignments:* Specify by assignments and practicum supervisor(s).

8. *Elementary or Secondary School Student Assistants:* Explain arrangement for released time and responsibilities.

9. *Professional Staff Other than Educators:* Include here,

for example, the school physician and any others, with duties and services supplied.

10. *Secretarial and Clerical Staff:* State nature of work to be done by each.

11. *Custodial Staff:* State nature of work to be done by each.

12. *Other Staff:* Use this heading or an elaboration for any staff not included above.

IV. *GENERAL EDUCATIONAL SPECIFICATIONS FOR THE SCHOOL:* This section orients the planners to the population and curricular parameters of the school (i.e. number of pupils, age range, comprehensive or limited purpose curriculum) and to the other characteristics the school is expected to have. Educational specifications are detailed statements of the educational activities to be carried out in a facility. They are an integral part of the education program. The best educational specifications are vivid, honest, and detailed. They emphasize what is typical or usual, although they also call attention to what can happen, what extremes the school space must be able to accommodate.

A. *Desired Atmosphere to be Created:* Here is discussed the feeling-tone which the structure should generate in pupils, staff, faculty, parents, and the general public.

B. *Common Characteristics of the Learning Areas:* Certain spaces in the school may be designated for music, science, or other particular learning experiences. Nevertheless, all learning spaces may have similarities. It is to those similarities, those common qualities, that this part of the educational specifications document speaks.

C. *Common Characteristics of Other Parts of the Structure:* All parts of a school should be designed to foster learning of a constructive kind. Color schemes, ceiling and floor treatments, amenities—these are examples of the components which should be the subject matter of this section. Focus on the *functional and performance characteristics* desired: resist the temptation to specify colors, specific floor finishes, and the like.

D. *Relationships of Curricular, Extra-curricular, and Management Functions to Each Other:* In this part of the Education Document the interactions among staff, faculty, administration, and pupils are highlighted. Here, too, the temptation to give specific directions must be avoided. To say, "Put the administrative offices beside the main entrance," or, "Put science areas next to music areas," is to give the architect directions rather than rationale. Instead, it is preferable to say in writing what educationally relevant interactions you desire to achieve. Thus, you allow the architect to understand what you want to accomplish and then give the architect the chance to attempt to organize the structural components to help achieve your educational objectives.

E. *External Characteristics of the Facility:* The educational activities envisioned for performance in the area immediately external to the building, the relationships of those educational activities to their counterparts inside the structure, the anticipated student movement flow, and the expected number and kinds of visitors are examples of information to be included under this heading.

V. *EDUCATIONAL SPECIFICATIONS FOR PARTICULAR LEARNING AREAS:* This section is based on the curricular organization of the school. Each element or unit of the actual curriculum to be offered (i.e. art, reading, social studies, etc.) should be identified as a subheading. Mathematics is used as an example below.

A. *Mathematics:* The curriculum should encompass the material usually taught to the pupils who have the characteristics in III-D above. In short, the curriculum should be consistent with the needs, capabilities, and expectations of the learners.

1. *Objectives:* This heading covers the purposes or expected outcomes of instruction in the curriculum.

2. *Learning Activities:* Here are listed the kinds of pupil-teacher and pupil-pupil activities to be encountered and the approximate proportions of each. The inde-

pendent study, small group study, individualized teaching, peer teaching, team teaching, and other activities should be described in sufficient detail to clarify what the typical daily learning activities will involve.

3. *Use of Movable Furniture and Equipment:* It should be pointed out again here that the writers of the educational specifications should avoid drawing plans for the architect. Instead, what needs to be specified is the *use* of the furniture and equipment rather than their placement or design. If it is going to be necessary to have large flat surfaces on which children can prepare charts and graphs; if individual work with an electrical computer demands twenty minutes per day for individual pupils on a demand basis; if Cuisinere Rods, blocks, or abaci are to be available for pupils to move from storage to use and back to storage, these are the kinds of information which should be included. It may help those preparing the educational specifications if they draft schematic pictures of their intended use of furniture and equipment. It may also be helpful if present available instructional space is *mocked-up* to test the desired procedures in the space being planned. But such exercises should be viewed as checklists to help assure that all the relevant information about educational activities is included rather than specific directions for the architect.

4. *General Considerations:* This catch-all heading can be used to note items in the educational program about mathematics which do not fit readily under other rubrics. For example, if the intention is to employ back-to-back scheduling with science so a common two period time block can be used one day a week or some other significant portion of the school year, that would belong here. If there are special problems with respect to noise, or light or noxious fumes, they can be pointed out here.

NOTE: The outline for mathematics illustrated above should be used with whatever necessary adaptations arise for all other curricular topics.

It should be remembered that *Special Education* is *not* a curricular topic comparable to *social studies* or *language arts.* If, however, there are certain topics (like a course in finding and keeping a job) which are specifically for certain groups of exceptional pupils, those topics should be designated by the course content titles and described here in terms of the pupil-teacher activities, the approximate amounts of each, and the kinds of instructional materials and approaches used.

It is important for the architect to be told the numbers and kinds of exceptional children to be expected in the pupil population. That would be covered under III-D above. Also, the architect needs to be made aware of the prevailing point of view about integration or segregation of those pupils. That should have been made clear in III-A above.

VI. *EDUCATIONAL SPECIFICATIONS FOR SPECIAL-IZED PROFESSIONAL SERVICES OR AREAS:* Some professional services like health services, guidance, or administration of the school are more easily described apart from the curricular topics as such, even though they interact. The same is true of certain areas like an auditorium or a cafeteria. This section of the document can be used to cover those services and areas.

A. *Administrative Services:* This includes the professional management of the school, the style of management, the way the management implements the school's goals; and this part of the narrative also describes the kinds of meetings, conferences, staff interactions, and other behaviors which are part of this group of services ranging from administering the school's policy to receiving and forwarding the mail.

B. *Instructional Planning:* In addition to carrying on planning at home and in the school's learning areas, teachers and others involved in instruction use opportunities to work with other teachers in planning or to have time to themselves for uninterrupted individual planning in the school facility. This section delineates the kinds of professional educational planning activities which will need to be carried on in the facility.

C. *Others:* Continue here with any additional specialized educational services or areas which need to be indicated.

The program can be concluded with a summary which restates in brief salient points or concepts. Also, it may be important to include appendices which are useful references. These may be the school system's manual for administrators, a copy of the collective bargaining contract with teachers, the board minutes regarding the school building program, the current school calendar, the directory of school employees, and other potentially relevant background material.

THE WORK MODULE

Robert L. Kahn coined the expression *work module*.[94] The work module represents the time period in which work is interesting, satisfying, uses the skills the worker possesses, and provides opportunity to increase present skills or acquire others. Work modules should be appropriate and fitting for the individual, should leave the worker unimpaired in the performance of other life roles at other than work times, and should supply rewards sufficient to justify to the worker continuing engagement in the tasks.

When children grow older, the work modules tend to become better defined and to occupy the worker longer. The following are estimates of work modules appropriate for different ages.

1. Birth to eighteen months: a few seconds up to thirty minutes. (i.e. feeding)
2. Eighteen months to thirty months: a few seconds to about five minutes. *One Minute*
3. Two and one-half years to four years: ten seconds to twenty minutes. *Five Minutes*
4. Four years to six years: thirty seconds to thirty minutes. *Ten Minutes*
5. Six years to nine years: five minutes to one hour. *Fifteen Minutes*

6. Nine years to thirteen years: ten minutes to two hours. *Twenty Minutes*

7. Thirteen years to eighteen years: twenty minutes to four hours. *Thirty Minutes*

The *median modules,* figures on the right are estimates of the amount of time children can usually be expected to devote to a school task before needing to turn from it to something else. This assumes that Kahn's criteria for a work module are met. Also, it will be necessary to adjust work module time to special educational considerations. For example, children who are very distractable can be expected to require shorter work modules at first.

Teachers and other professional educators, aides and assistants, and volunteers will operate in terms of work modules. The three broad categories of work modules for the instructional and support staff are:

1. Direct interface with individual children or very small groups of two or three including tutoring, conferring, testing, giving directions, planning, and arranging instructional space.

2. Instruction of larger groups of children of approximately thirty at a time.

3. Activities not involving direct contact with children but including possible interactions with adults such as consultants, other faculty members, or parents, as well as solitary recording, planning, and development.

Type 1. usually varies in length from three or four minutes to approximately twenty minutes per module. Type 2. tends to be longer than 1., varying between twenty minutes to eighty minutes. Types 1. and 2. occur mainly during the hours from 8:30 or 9:00 A.M. through 2:30 or 3:30 P.M. when pupils are in school. Type 3. modules take place chiefly in the earlier morning and the later afternoon hours in the school facility but can include designated planning time and preparation or conference periods scheduled regularly into the time pupils are in attendance.

The planning for instruction needs to recognize that work modules for pupils and staff will most frequently occur in the same space during the same time. The educational facility will need to accommodate itself to both adults and children pursuing work modules simultaneously and often jointly as in Types 1. and 2., as well as the adult only modules of Type 3.

CRITERIA FOR EDUCATION PROGRAM STRUCTURE

How can you ascertain whether the education program document is carrying the information and conveying the tone it should? One way is to reread it and to ask others to read it with certain criteria in mind.

We believe the following eight criteria should be met by any school's educational program. Perhaps you would want to modify them or add to them. Our criteria are:

1. The program should permit and encourage flexible grouping within and among disciplines as well as age levels.
2. Pupils should be grouped heterogeneously within instructional sections or special activities.
3. Provision should be made for special interest, enrichment, and exploratory activities with positive efforts by the faculty to effect participation by all pupils.
4. Instructional planning time should be provided in a carefully structured pattern for faculty and pupils.
5. A personal advisement and counseling program should be developed with focus on teacher-pupil relationships.
6. The school program should provide a satisfying and profitable academic, social, and personal experience for children.
7. The school program should effect a smooth transition in the level of education in which each child is found upon entry, proceeds through all the succeeding higher levels, and subsequently leaves the program.
8. The faculty should be encouraged to exercise initiative and creativity through a flexible and cooperatively planned instructional program.

Those criteria appear equally acceptable for any form of school. They furnish a reintroduction to the basic principles of the educational program preparation which are developed in more detail in what follows.

PURPOSE OF DETAILED SPECIFICATIONS

The architect needs to know to what uses the educator intends to

put space. That information is conveyed in a general sense by labels
such as *mathematics classroom* or *gymnasium* or *teachers' work area*.
Such general information is broadly helpful in deciding on probable
locations. For example, certain places are better for auditoriums or
gymnasiums than others. But to be as helpful as possible, the architect needs much more detailed data about the functions to be served
by the space being planned.

The educator's detailed educational specifications are conveyed more
clearly if they are in operational language. For example, it is important for the architect to know that pupils will study drama in
the language arts program. But it is more important for the architect
to know whether the study of drama will be done by reading from
books, by reviewing films, by rehearsing and playing scenes, or by
some combining of these or other approaches. The space, storage,
and lighting conditions, for instance, differ markedly for each of
those instructional procedures. Therefore, the more operationally
stated the educational specifications can be, the more likely it is
that the architect can match space and facilities to pupils' needs
and teachers' instructional styles. And that makes the difference
between neutral, uninspiring, and uninvolved space and a participating environment which helps teachers to teach and pupils to learn.

LEGAL AND REGULATORY SPECIFICATIONS

Unlike most other countries, the U.S.A. has laws or regulations
governing the design and constitution of school facilities which are
not centralized. Each state and territory, plus the District of Co-
lumbia, has its own legal specifications.

States have various cubic foot and square foot specifications for
space per pupil, for study areas, or for congregate areas such as
auditoriums or cafeterias. There may even be specifications conflicts
for such areas between state regulations and city ordinances.

Some states have cost ceilings. An imaginary example might be
phrased as follows: "The state reserves the right to require a local
referendum if a new school is projected to cost more than twenty-
eight hundred dollars per pupil for elementary schools, four thousand
dollars per pupil for middle or junior high schools, and more than
fifty-two hundred dollars per pupil for senior high schools."

The legal specifications and their relation to the educational program need to be stated so they are clear at the outset to the educational and architectural planners. Knowing the legal conditions can help avoid costly changes which could be necessitated if they are overlooked. Also, if certain important innovative ideas of the educator-architect team call for alterations in local or state standards, the possibilities for securing variances need to be checked with proper authorities immediately.

CHAPTER XII

THE ARCHITECTURAL RESPONSE

A dictum of contemporary architecture is that form should follow function. In other words, a building should look like what it does. There is no reason, for instance, why an airport terminal should look like a hospital or the reverse. In fact, such dissonance in appearance would very probably be accompanied by problems of efficiency and effectiveness in actual use.

But form can follow function in school structures only if the functions are plainly spelled out in language the architect finds readily understandable. And the function must be explicated in all possible detail.

THE ARCHITECT'S ADVISORY COMMITTEE

Community representatives need to be in direct and continuing contact with the architect who is designing the school that their children and their friends' children will attend. One primary objective of discussions between the architect and community representatives is to assure that they exchange ideas about the general character and design of the school. A second is to help the architect arrange the school so that parents and other patrons can be a part of it and feel as much at home there as the teachers and administrators do. A third reason is to obtain added direct input from community activities which need to be housed or accommodated in the school building. A fourth reason is to implement another channel of community communication during a time when a very significant educational move is being made which will affect everyone.

Members of the teaching, supervisory, and administrative group associated with the projected school and with similar schools should serve on the advisory committee, too. They are needed chiefly to give even more detailed interpretations to the educational requirements of the building than can be supplied readily in writing or by the staff of educational planners. Also, it is important that they react directly to ideas that the architect believes might be answers to particular space use issues.

The advisory committee for each school should be formed by action of the superintendent and the community representatives. The formation of such an advisory committee should start at the very outset of the total planning process for each school.

Each public school, especially those which accommodate handicapped pupils, is one of the most complex organisms in American society. Such a school has a life of its own which influences and is influenced by the vital substances of the community which flow around and through it.

A new or remodeled school presents its patrons with significant opportunities to make their community stronger and to lead it to a higher level of development and civilization. To achieve that large purpose, of course, it is necessary to infuse the budding schools, from the first moment of planning, with the ideas of the people in the community, with a strong and well-prepared staff, a rich instructional program, inviting space for instruction, and freedom of action at the local level sufficient to blend the other characteristics into a responsible and effective force for education.

DETERMINING THE NEED TO BUILD OR REMODEL

In simplistic terms, the most acceptable reasons to build or to remodel are proof that (a) there are too many children for the available facilities to accommodate, or (b) the available facilities are unsafe. Less readily acceptable but still within reason is a third contingency: the available facilities, though large and safe enough, are not suitable for housing educational programs of good quality. The last is also the most difficult to prove.

How can the determination best be made? It can be done by what educators simply call a *needs assessment*. It asks the question, "What is needed to provide the sound education anyone deserves?" not, "What is the absolute minimum?" Most citizens are not willing to settle for that, for they want their children to fare better than they did. Similarly, it doesn't ask, "What is the most luxurious?" Americans and most others in the world that we have talked to feel that it is possible to overdo. An excellent school has a functional quality of its own which excites admiration. A gift of love like the Taj Mahal is a thing of beauty in its own right, but it is clearly not a school building.

So the *needs assessment* is an important early step. And it can be conducted quite simply. A questionnaire is often the instrument of choice for that purpose. Consultation should be sought from special educators, architects, and professional planners, also. The result should be hard, convincing data, data which indicates what construction or remodeling needs to be done and why.

It is important in this connection, also, to remember to ask teachers, pupils, and parents for their ideas. They have many good ideas, and they tend to be quite practical.

MINOR MODIFICATIONS IN CONVENTIONAL BUILDINGS

It is feasible to move some traditional buildings into the modern day by changes which can be modest in cost.

Temporary Classrooms

When rapid expansion, temporary expansion, auxiliary space for special projects, or other similar conditions call for quickly increased instructional areas, temporary classrooms should be considered along with other alternatives.

Excellent use was recently made of such units in Ashtabula County, Ohio. The region is sparsely populated and low in socio-economic level. Available school facilities were extensively used and left little space which could be used for the special education programs which were acknowledged to be needed. Within a year from the point of decision, a dozen prefabricated schoolrooms were linked to existing schools in various parts of the county, and the needed special education programs were operative.

There has sometimes been a tendency to use temporary, add-on buildings for classroom space for handicapped children and to leaving the basic structure for use by regular classes. That is a sure way to draw attention to the separateness of the special education program from that of the rest of the pupils. It is our view that special education children and regular class children should share equally in the use of any temporary facilities as another means of emphasizing the equality of educational opportunities of all pupils and of illustrating the shared responsibilities all pupils and teachers accept.

Space Reassignment

In both the Wyomissing (Pa.) Middle School and the Sacred Heart Parish (Pa.) Middle School, a new focus on individualized education was achieved without tearing down walls and making the whole school one classroom.[146]

> Instead, learning stations were placed along inner walls of classrooms, and tables were arranged for small-group study and instruction. At Wyomissing Middle School, halls became places to learn without interrupting the normal flow of traffic. Corners, alcoves, storage areas, and closets were also turned over to students. (Space-use changes such as these should be checked against safety and fire standards, of course.) At Sacred Heart, halls were too narrow to accommodate learning, but two vacant rooms were pressed into service.

The teachers in the schools took active part in the redesign of the learning space. Much of the work was done as a service at nearby Millersville State College. The enterprise was lubricated by $125,000 in federal grant funds. F. Perry Love, a Millersville staff member, directed the project.

Love feels that, "The less formal atmosphere will produce more positive student attitudes about school, fewer failures, and less pressure."

For those students who cannot learn without constant direction, there are conventional teaching provisions in both schools to make such pupils feel secure.

As students become more responsible they are given progressively more freedom: the freedom of being allowed to leave the group to study independently in a classroom, then to leave the classroom to study independently in a hallway or some other area of the building. Teachers can then give their attention to slow learners or students who cannot work independently.

DETERMINING THE CHARACTER OF A SCHOOL

There is often a temptation to predetermine the chief design features of a school for the architect rather than to present him with the purposes, objectives, and activities and allow him to exert his artistry and skill in developing space to complement those purposes, objectives, and activities. High quality results more often occur if that temptation is resisted. To specify to the architect at the outset that, "The school is to be divided into separate and distinct halls arranged around a central core or hub," or to tell him that, "This must be a triangle, with administration at one apex, common facilities at another, and the facilities for the handicapped at the third," will not usually save time or effort and, even if that is its goal, it could result in a very unsatisfactory design. The educational specifications most helpful to the architect are, instead, couched in language which clarifies the educational procedures and operations to be carried out in that space.

The architect and the educator need to share a check list of organizing principles and practices which they agree will be designed into the school. It is on these organizing principles that instructional planning and space planning must reach a compatible interface. If successfully accomplished, space design then complements teaching style, and instruction is strengthened because of the setting in which it occurs.

Below are key educational principles and practices which we believe should form the backbone of any school which is to include handicapped pupils.

Scheduling Specifications Are Unique. It makes a real difference to both architect and educator if the instructional space is expected to respond simply to seven equal periods a day or to a module of twenty minutes and its multiples. Also, it makes a difference if class sessions in science and mathematics are expected to operate independently or if teaching areas are to be arranged so science and mathematics teachers can combine groups in a variety of ways for team teaching.

The school which includes handicapped pupils should operate as close as possible to the beginning and closing times determined by general practices in the community and school system in which it is located. However, the needs of some children may require earlier starts and later stops in the school day for certain pupils and teachers, and the school design must accommodate to those requirements. The internal daily schedule should also be planned to fit the needs of the particular school. Usually, it is a six or seven period day so far as the broad structure of the schedule is concerned. However, each school should be authorized to develop a daily plan which suits the requirements of the community, the pupils, and the teachers, and which encourages modular, block-of-time, and back-to-back scheduling.

As an example, a useful schedule pattern for the elementary, middle, or high school day consists of eighteen instructional modules, each of twenty minutes duration. The schedule of modules use is designed by the local school staff. Great ranges of schedule design are available, based on the multiples of a single module. The twenty-minute time is usually the shortest meaningful exposure to a topic or learning task, although it can be broken into five or ten minute units if desired. A single module of twenty minutes is effective for large group presentations, small group discussions, a developmental or remedial reading session, or a counseling session. Two modules, forty minutes, allow in-depth work in English, mathematics, or science; while three or four modules, sixty to eighty minutes at a stretch, accommodate project work, independent study, or activities calling for extensive laboratory setups. Modular scheduling permits day-to-day alterations as needed for differentiated curricula.

A *block-of-time* is made up of two or more twenty-minute modules. Block-of-time scheduling encourages team teaching, interrelating of subjects, and varying the size of pupil groups for instruction. An example might be the scheduling of English in an eighty-minute block for all sixth graders. The group of teachers involved then could organize and reorganize instruction in modules within that time block from day to day and deploy themselves in ways best designed to accomplish their various instructional objectives. Block-of-time scheduling also encourages *back-to-back* scheduling, an aid to teaching material related to two fields such as science and mathematics or art and music. In back-to-back block-of-time scheduling, for example, mathematics should be scheduled for the same forty-minute block each day and science for another forty-minute block each day immediately before or immediately following mathematics. Then the mathematics and science teachers could work as a team to plan how best to use part or all of the time available to help pupils attain instructional objectives.

School Instruction Will Be Varied. Many different instructional systems and approaches are now being applied successfully in schools at all levels in preschool through high school, and there are certainly more to come. The rapid increase of commercially developed instructional systems with attendant hardware and software means that every school needs to have the potentiality for flexibility in use of teaching areas, ample space for instructional materials storage and retrieval, and a staff and a set of procedures which assure ready and effective use of those materials.

Teaching Space in Schools Is Different in Appearance from the boxlike classrooms which many of today's parents remember. The difference results from improvements in the manner that education is provided for pupils.

The appearance of the western world's classrooms remained essentially unchanged for three hundred years. Imprinted indelibly on generations was the oblong room with high silled windows along at least one side. The teacher's domain was at the front. Except for minor alterations in chalkboard color and placement and in the nature of the pupils' seats, the pattern was fixed.

The style of the room reflected the style of the teaching. With rare exceptions the *class* was taught as a whole with the same books, charts, and other instructional materials. There is evidence now, however, of an increased amount of individualization and small group work in all grades in more recent years. It has been enough in most places to result in loosening the seats from the floor, and, in some places, in changing the configuration of the room itself.

The improvements in teaching know-how which first pressed the primary grades toward individualization two or three decades ago now have avalanched through the middle years of schooling, spilling their influence even into the high school grades. The result is a new way of thinking about the space in which teaching takes place.

Most areas of the school are used for instruction at some time. The idea that teaching takes place only in separate classrooms has given way to space planning which encourages instruction for individuals or groups in almost any portion of the building. The building itself is a teaching device that should be used.

Individualized independent study is encouraged by placing carrels and study corners at convenient places throughout the structure. Each month there are more good, individualized, self-administering study packages coming into the school market. That means buildings must be adaptable in the direction of being able to add more individual study settings over the years ahead.

First generation open space is essential in the design of school teaching areas. It will be necessary in order to encourage easy shifts from large group to small group spaces and to make feasible the use of some large and some small teaching areas in varying combinations from day to day.

Free learning environment approaches call for adaptable space, and those approaches give promise of increasing usefulness.

Homogeneous Groupings of New Kinds Are Used in Schools. They are based on interest and pupil learning style in addition to achievement and aptitude. Thus, certain children from different grades may be guided to work together in designing and constructing a botanical garden because their teachers know that those particular pupils are challenged most and learn best while in the process of drawing and digging and building rather than through reading or watching. Other children from the same or different grades may practice vocal or instrumental songs exemplifying the ethnic backgrounds of the community as part of social studies. The kind of grouping and regrouping which this illustrates is a far cry from the more rigid *tracking* concept which characterized the relatively inflexible homogeneous groupings of past decades.

Flexibility of Pupil Progress Is An Important Quality. The principal and the faculty should have the authority and should be encouraged to arrange for children to take courses on multiple grade levels. Some seventh grade children are so capable in mathematics or English, for example, that they might well take eighth grade courses in addition to or instead of the seventh grade offerings. Similar adjustments can be made for pupils who have weaknesses which might be remedied by reviewing courses or parts of courses previously taken.

In this connection, it is expected that there will be an increasing number of minicourses or miniunits which run for shorter than usual periods of time. Other specially arranged courses, too, which are not normally part of the system wide curriculum will be developed and offered in particular schools.

Schools will have no architectural barriers to the handicapped. Schools will meet the standards which assure full access to their educational, recreational, and social facilities for handicapped children, teachers, parents, and other citizens. This goes beyond the ordinary and by now widely accepted standards relating to general access and movement within the building. School buildings will also have more sophisticated features which will allow handicapped pupils and other persons, professionals, or support staff to work or to socialize readily in the structure and to have available all the amenities needed by anyone. By the same token, there will be full use of the building by handicapped pupils from the attendance area unless there are compelling reasons for the handicapped pupils to attend a special school. In short, architectural barriers to access, mobility, or daily life routines will not be allowed to prevent handicapped parents from visiting their children's schools, nor to prevent the employment of otherwise qualified handicapped persons, nor be allowed to be a reason why handicapped children may not attend school with their neighbors.

The directed activities program is designed to help each student develop the study and work behaviors characteristic of individuals who achieve a high degree of academic success. When each pupil knows that his and the teacher's purpose go far beyond just getting an assignment done, it is a vast improvement over the study hall of the past. Instead, each pupil knows that the directed activities area is designed to put within his reach the materials and the teacher advice which should move him forward in learning how to learn more effectively.

Social events are a significant part of ongoing pupil life in all schools. Space considerations which relate to social events are as follows:

1. The entire school should be able to assemble to view programs presented live on stage.

2. One group at a time should be able to have a party which includes food service, group games, contests, group singing, and square and other folk dancing.
3. It should be possible to separate a party area from the rest of the school so that:
    a. a noisy party could be held without interfering with study groups and other meetings in the school at the same time, or
    b. it could be held after school hours, and the areas of the school other than those in use for the party would be inaccessible.

The sophistication level of social events and the nature of social activities are to be determined largely by the pupils' age levels and community desires and standards. Also, social events will recognize and encourage the understanding of the different cultures of the community served by the school.

Students need opportunities to exercise self-government and to participate in the governance of the entire school. Students, depending on their ages, can be expected to be involved in:

1. Selection and management of extra-curricular activities.
2. Planning and conducting schoolwide social and cultural events.
3. Development of the school's curriculum.
4. Design of the schedules of classes.

In order to assure the accomplishment of substantial and continuing student involvement, it is necessary to assign appropriate space for the use of student groups and their officers and committees.

Teachers' office space needs to be clustered so that several can readily work together. At the same time, teachers' office space should allow privacy for professional matters and for those personal matters which are essential even in the work setting.

Some cooperative teacher planning will be within academic subjects. For instance, all of the social studies teachers will sometimes need to get together, or all of the science teachers will need to get together. In some instances, all of the subject teachers from a group of several grades will need to meet together for planning or development or research purposes.

Also, it must be easy for teachers to meet and discuss matters of mutual concern across academic subjects. The foreign language and social studies teachers, for instance, may work with the health and physical education teachers in planning local simulations of historic or contemporary Olympic games or with the reading teachers on study skills. More frequently, perhaps, back-to-back scheduling of mathematics and science or English and social studies will foster meetings between those pairs of teacher groups to plan educational programs for students.

The influence of the above educational factors can be expected to pervade today's and tomorrow's school. It is expected that that influence will have a major impact on the design of all the educational elements of the structure.

ENRICHMENT OF THE SCHOOL ENVIRONMENT BY ART OBJECTS

High quality original art works are appearing more often in schools in America. Works by Hans Arp, Picasso, Henry Moore, and others are not uncommon in European schools and other public buildings. Funds for such elements in schools are routinely provided in several European countries. The same level of appreciation has not been reached in the United States, but there is a beginning. The Elementary and Secondary Education Act of 1965 provided that, "Architects may include works of art costing no more than one percent of the total cost of construction and site development." Judicious use of funds, even under that limitation, can result in enhancement of the aesthetic quality of the learning environment.

An added advantage of making original art of high quality an integral part of the school setting is the opportunity it affords the pupils in understanding the daily life and work of the artist. The stimulation of contemplating careers in the creative arts is an essential part of broad-based career education.

THE SCHOOL'S APPEARANCE

Each school should be an example of excellence in appearance and character. The school, both inside and outside, should reflect the achievements and aspirations of pluralistic American society. It should be a product of today's cultures and, at the same time, a friendly and helpful beacon for children on their way into their own futures.

It should possess a beauty which grows out of the functional harmony between its objectives and its setting.

New or remodeled school environments should excite the imagination of both adults and children. Each structure should be replete with magnetic challenges to the visitors and attract patrons and students to exert their abilities in constructive ways. Also, schools should offer amicable, nonthreatening responses to the concerns and interests of those who approach and enter their doors.

The main function of the school building and its surrounding area is to provide an appealing and helpful environment for learning. Therefore, space, movement, comfort, and esthetic appeal are all significant. The plant should be comfortable, easy to maintain, and safe. The total design should be bold and imaginative and proclaim the identity of the school.

Those desired effects will not result from expensive adornments unrelated to the true nature of the structure. Each new school is first of all a school, and each should show its real character by its physical appearance and by the activities which meet the eye of anyone entering it. Efficiency and effectiveness of operation are functional determinants of the kind of grace and refinement desired in the building.

The long lesson of history has shown us that whenever we have attempted to build eternal, imperishable things, they turn out to be either difficult and irrational to use, gray, hard, and repelling to people; or gloriously beautiful (i.e. the Taj Mahal) but with little functional value. The school should do what our larger society has to do: be ready to encompass a rich diversity of behavior and cultural input. This includes our peripheral members: the handicapped, the deprived, and the brilliant. As a critical model, it should be the aim of the school to keep a live exploration under way. "How big, colorful, and diverse are we?"

There is a national cliche of asking children what they are going to be when they grow up: as if they weren't somebody and something already. How do we discover who we are and how we function in society? It is by practical experience which is both personal and vicarious. The vehicles for practicing social, intellectual, and physical skills are study, simulation, play, and games; and the school should abound in opportunities for them. Again, we will have to make a deliberate investment in time and place if our schools are to serve as social arenas or cause and effect places that are rich in feedback.

The nonverbal content of our surroundings is compelling. We act very much as we are directed to by the tone and quality of our physical environment. A school facility delivers a tonal message to its inhabitants, and this has important potential. It can, as it all too often does, present a tough, defensive, "I can take anything you can hit me with" message. We should recognize that the student can be expected, indeed, to deliver the subsequent assault in response to that stimulus.

What kinds of total objectives should be sought in a school facility?

To be unself-conscious.

To be human scaled, welcoming and approachable.

To be warm, a growing place.

To be economic, reasonable, accountable.

To be usable, consumable, and capable of regeneration.

A school that is habitable and humane gains in return the moderate, happy behavior of people who like where they are.

COSTS OF SCHOOL CONSTRUCTION

In 1960, the average cost of building a school in Pennsylvania was $2,304 per pupil occupancy rated. In 1972, that cost was $4,453 per pupil.

These figures include all elementary and secondary buildings lumped together and averaged. There is no way to sift out what the costs were per special education pupil.

It is obvious, however, that per pupil special education building costs must be higher than the costs for other pupils. The main reason is that each special education pupil on the average requires twice as much space in terms of square feet of floor as does the typical pupil. Special instructional equipment, wheelchairs and mobility aids, equipment for helping sight and hearing: these and other necessary materials result in taking up more space. Since school construction costs are usually reported in terms of square footage of space and since handicapped pupils are assigned approximately double the usual amount of space as other pupils, the cost can be roughly estimated as double.

CONSTRUCTION STANDARDS

School board members and architects must live with the buildings they produce. The structures are constant reminders of the thought that goes into them. It is understandable that both board members and architects would want their work to stand up well under the examination of succeeding generations of pupils and taxpayers for whom the facilities were designed and constructed.

A good future for a school building can best be assured if everyone agrees at the outset that its quality standards will be high. We believe that this applies whether it is a major building or a modest remodeling.

Setting high standards is not synonymous with setting expensive standards. It demands seeking out preferred practices and making them prevailing practices. It is reasonable to expect that high quality in a structure will result in an excellent cost/effectiveness ratio rather than result in a situation in which a great deal of money is spent with minimal return in school and community usefulness. Application of high standards should encourage the development of a school which gives a maximum return in usefulness for each dollar spent and which provides safe and sound structure whose presence in the community is enriching to the spirit.

LEARNING TO USE INSTRUCTIONAL SPACE

The educational staff must have instruction in how to make optimum use of the school facility. Even when an architect is sensitive to the needs of potential users and achieves a creative and functional design, his design's best instructional features are not automatically put to good use.

In 1972, Probst [133] said the following in a discussion of the open high school,

> Flexible design has little to do with flexible use. Teachers and administrators must learn to think like designers. They must approach open space in terms of the manipulation of subspaces. Traffic and communication effect has to be incorporated into their thinking. And since change and motion are central to the open school, all this means quite frankly that management of the environment must become an ongoing process. It must become a familiar tool used with the same kind of purpose and validity as teaching itself. This calls for new roles and responsibilities.

We know at first hand of a facility designed for the education of handicapped pupils where a significant amount of floor space, about one twenty-fifth, of the school was set aside for a certain function. The teacher-administrator-architect team prepared the area as a wet room to allow, even encourage, the use of water, clay, and other water-soluble materials to be used particularly by trainable retarded pupils. The square foot cost for that unit was relatively high compared to equivalent space in other parts of the building because it had walls and floors which, while safe, were also water- and stain-resistant so that the door could be closed and the room could actually be washed down by a hose.

Key teachers and administrators who planned the facility moved before the building opened. The new staff knew generally what the room was for, but they had not participated in designing it. So when the principal found the custodian resistant to the special chore of keeping the *wet room* in usable condition, its special purpose was forgotten. Now used to accommodate the custodian's supplies, it could well be the most expensive storage closet in any building in the region.

In a case in which all the children attending a special school were brought by bus, a 10-foot by 12-foot space adjacent to the loading area was enclosed and furnished as a headquarters for transient bus drivers and aides. A telephone was provided for any communications needs. Lavatories were also included. After a year, it was found that the space was never used. Drivers and aides seldom left the buses. The space is now used to store outdoor play equipment, especially that which cannot be used in the winter months.

Good management suggests that the educator-architect team which creates a facility have follow-up roles in its use. School plants will be improved in the future as will the capabilities of architects if their commissions call for brief review and utilization studies at one, two, and five year intervals after initial occupancy. At the same time, teachers and others responsible for schools might well consider periodic reviews of the educational programs on which the facilities in which they teach were designed. Professional competencies could be sharpened by such in-service activities, and more fruitful uses might well be evolved for the everyday settings in which instruction is conducted.

EARLY CHILDHOOD EDUCATION

Recognition of the importance of systematic teaching and encouragement during the first four or five years of life has produced another new thrust in special education. It started with special nursery and kindergarten arrangements for handicapped children. The movement now includes guidance for parents in stimulating their infants and toddlers long before the usual nursery school age.

One emphasis during the early childhood years is on the prevention of deprivation. Crippled children who might otherwise be immobile are helped to move into a normal range of contacts with their environment. Similarly, blind children, deaf children, and retarded children are bombarded with stimuli to minimize the effect of their sensory or intellectual limitations.

This means that there could be staff members of the school system who would go to the homes of handicapped babies and toddlers on a regular schedule of perhaps once or twice a week for an hour or more of instruction of the parents and child together. It also means that there could be a need for special education for infants, toddlers, and other preschoolers as part of any day care centers in the school system's attendance area. Also, there could be periodic meetings at the school of parents with their infants, toddlers, or other preschoolers. The meetings could vary in size. One might be a cluster of four or five parents who would work together on a special activity such as learning about the toy lending library. Another might be a group of twenty or thirty who would see an orientation film as the infant swimming lessons were being conducted in the school pool.

In addition, there might need to be a facility at the school to which telephone calls could be made by parents any time of the day or night to get assistance with training problems. And there might be the need for production of a weekly newsletter to parents of young children.

Appropriate facilities might also be needed for the preschoolers old enough to receive aggregate instruction at school for two to six hours per day. These might be complicated by the need for special paraeducational help, physical, occupational, or speech therapies, or special preventive and corrective tutoring in perception or mobility.

It is hoped that the above illustrations are enough to make two points clear. First, there is an emerging set of activities regarding very early childhood education for handicapped pupils which is very complex and which can be different in many important ways from what has traditionally been called nursery and kindergarten schooling. Second, there is a need for creative architectural solutions for the best ways to use space to foster excellent programs of instruction.

Flexibility will certainly be as important here as it would in any program in a developing state. But it is not sufficient to simply say, "Give us a lot of flexible space because we're not sure how we'll use it." Rather, it is much more desirable to include as many examples of actual possibilities for the use of the space as can be realistically envisioned in the educational program when it is actually being written and submitted to the architect. That will, in all probability, guide both the architect and the educator to a result which will be much more satisfactory for those who will need to use it in the future.

THE FUTURE OF THE SCHOOL BUILDING

School buildings over the years reflect alterations in the nature of public education as well as the larger changes in society. Factors of great significance to school buildings in today's more crowded and expensive life are site practicability and the possibilities for multiple use of public structures.

Multistory Buildings

Schools of the future may need more and more to be multistory buildings. That condition is dictated by topography, site availability, and cost of land. Large level areas are scarce: many are already in use. The high cost of city and suburban real estate is another factor which makes it very unlikely that there will be many opportunities to have schools built in the meandering, one-level pattern so common in the recent past.

Multistory buildings generally are more costly to construct than those on one level. The reasons include the need for higher strength standards for foundations and structural members, loss of functional space due to stairwells and elevator shafts, and the like. Therefore, comparisons of costs with existing buildings must take account of the multistory factor as well as other factors which bring about increases.

Joint Occupancy

To avoid burdening the tax base with the entire cost of a new school, land and air space can be occupied jointly by a school and an income producing enterprise. Joint occupancy is a method of cutting the cost of schools. It is being tested in several parts of the United States.

One approach is to build to accommodate housing, retail stores, or office space. The result, usually, is a single structure or complex of mixed and private uses, all jointly designed, constructed, and operated. The ideal is to include enough taxpaying commercial space to carry the cost of debt service on the school.

A different approach is to combine schools and other public facilities. Public libraries, day-care centers, health facilities, community colleges, welfare and social service agencies, cultural and recreational facilities all can mix well with schools.

Shared multiple use and joint construction can produce substantial savings in land and building costs and can lead to more productive use of the facilities.

School districts today cannot afford to overlook any possibilities which could produce improved human services and higher productivity for each construction dollar spent.

ILLUSTRATIONS OF EXCELLENT DESIGN

In a number of instances, we have been privileged to have major responsibility for the design of schools and schooling for handicapped pupils, of regular schools, and of combined schools. In other cases, we have had the good fortune to serve as consultants to those with design and construction responsibility. Those experiences have taken us into many parts of the United States.

In addition, we have visited and made intensive studies of literally dozens of specialized schools which were originally designed or remodeled to include handicapped pupils. Some were almost a century old, while others still smelled of fresh plaster, wood, and concrete.

Some were contemporary architectural prizewinners, and others did not reach that level.

Our studies of schools took us to all parts of the world. We do not believe our visits to twenty-five countries have made us experts on the schools and schooling of each. Far from it! We have observed, however, the great variety of approaches taken across the world to this serious problem, and we have tried to distill from those observations some principles to guide what we would say here.

One thing we decided *not* to do is present specific models for school systems to copy. We made that decision for three reasons:

1. We found no model schools which would fit all situations, even with modest modifications.
2. There are examples of well-designed schools, facilities, and equipment already described in publications which are readily available.
3. We are convinced that significant educational and community development accompanies the creative activities associated with designing schools and schooling locally, as opposed to copying a design from elsewhere or accepting a design imposed by higher authorities.

Those three reasons would probably suffice in themselves. But it is also true that special education operates in a continuing state of developmental change. The same is true, though to a lesser extent, of education in general, the great context in which special education resides. The growth and modification of special education is very active: so active that to present specific models of structures in detail would be less useful to the reader than to present principles and examples as we have attempted to do.

THEN AND NOW

In the fifteenth century, schools were accepted as places which offered education on a take it or leave it basis. The pupils or families paid for the opportunity of school attendance but had nothing to say about the content of the curriculum or the teacher's methods. Pupils could accept the service of the school or not; the school had little responsibility beyond that.

Since the nineteenth century, the school's job has changed. Now it is expected to try to motivate children and youth to become educated. Now it is expected to adapt school offerings to each child's particular requirements.

The new rule for the schools has altered the way schools are designed and built. Changes in function wrought changes in structure. Pictures of ancient schools tell what they were. The layouts of modern schools speak about what they are. The choice is ours.

BIBLIOGRAPHY

BASIC REFERENCES FOR THE DESIGN TEAM

In view of our conclusion not to present specific design models, we decided also to present no sketches or plans in this book. Instead, we offer our recommendations and comments on a basic library of references. These are books and articles we believe would be most useful for the educators, architects, school board members, and other citizens who will be seriously involved in the design of schools and schooling for the handicapped.

Environmental Design: A New Relevance for Special Education is the title of a 1971 publication of The Council for Exceptional Children, 1411 South Jefferson Davis Highway, Arlington. Alan Abeson was the project coordinator and Julie Blacklow the author.

The 120-page book has four chapters. The first offers recommendations and describes the findings of a national investigation of existing facilities in which exceptional children are taught. A key finding, and one on which we have dwelt throughout this book, was that "Minor modifications in the teacher's own working space can markedly improve the environment and ultimately the program."

A second finding was that "Teachers have often been denied the opportunity to participate in the planning of the school buildings in which they work."

A third finding is that "There is a need for staff evaluation of school buildings." It was pointed out in connection with this finding that educators need training aimed at making them aware of environmental effects and environmental modifications.

Two other points are emphasized. One is that special educators with little background in planning and designing facilities do not expect enough from architects, with the result that the buildings which are developed are ineffective. Second, teachers and other educators must inform the architect fully about what instructional related demands are going to be made on the structure. That information given to the architect (through the education program or planning

[205]

narrative) should be in rich detail and stated explicitly in plain language, point by point.

Notably helpful is the second chapter on planning, progress, and people. It features comments, often quite practical and illustrative of preferred practices, by the following.

Frank Hewett, Chairman, Program in Special Education, University of California, Los Angeles, California.

Donald Blodgett, Executive Director, Department of Exceptional Education and Special Programs, Milwaukee Public Schools, Wisconsin.

Charles Woodcook, Superintendent, School for the Blind, Salem, Oregon.

Sidney Eisenshtat, Architect, Beverly Hills, California.

Ralph Baird, Director, Department of Special Education, Tacoma Public Schools, Washington.

Richard Veenstra, Architect, Jacksonville, Florida.

Alan Abeson, Project Coordinator, The Council for Exceptional Children, Arlington, Virginia.

Bertram Berenson, Dean, School of Architecture, University of Nebraska, Lincoln, Nebraska.

William Cruickshank, Director, Institute for the Study of Mental Retardation and Related Disabilities, University of Michigan, Ann Arbor, Michigan.

Herbert C. Quay, Chairman, Division of Educational Psychology, Temple University, Philadelphia, Pennsylvania.

The third chapter deals with verbal and graphic solutions. It contains twenty-one drawings with accompanying text, addressed to a variety of problems from surfaces to storage.

The last chapter by Clifford Drew of the University of Utah at Salt Lake City deals with research having to do with environmental manipulation. Suggestions are made for possible applications.

Designing for the Handicapped is the title of a 1971 publication of George Godwin, Limited, 4 Catherine St., London, W C 2. It was edited by Kenneth Bayes, an architect who is also a consultant to the British Department of Health and Social Security, and by Sandra Franklin, a designer conducting research at the Medical Architecture Research Institute, Northern Polytechnic, London.

Authors of the several chapters each tend to devote modest time to the fundamental issues involved in designing for a particular handicap. The chapters vary in the degree to which they are theoretical and abstract as opposed to being operational and specific. The following topics are included, often with helpful drawings, sketches, or photos.

1. "Introduction," N. E. Bank-Mikkelsen, Director of the Department of Mental Retardation Services of the Danish National Board of Social Welfare.
2. "The Handicapped and Their Needs," Kenneth Bayes and Sandra Franklin.
3. "Design Approach to An Individual Building," Kenneth Bayes and Sandra Franklin.
4. "The Therapeutic Environment," Kenneth Bayes and Sandra Franklin.
5. "The Mildly Mentally Subnormal," Ivan Nellist, Architect, England.
6. "The Mentally Ill," Humphrey Osmond, Director, Bureau of Research in Neurology and Psychiatry, Princeton, New Jersey; and Kyo Izumi, Chairman, Human Information and Ecology Programme, University of Saskatchewan.
7. "Maladjusted Children," Jane Hough, Architect and Consultant to the New York Health Services and Administration.
8. "The Blind and the Partially Sighted," G. R. Adams, Architect, England.
9. "The Deaf and Partially Hearing," L. W. Bates, Architect, Research in Design for the Deaf, University of Sheffield.
10. "Learning Disability," Bertram Berenson, Dean, School of Architecture, University of Nebraska.
11. "Gifted Children," Eric Heaf, Lecturer, Department of Architecture, University of Sheffield.
12. "Environment for Assessment," Kenneth S. Holt, Director, Wolfson Center, Department of Developmental Paediatrics, Institute of Child Health, London.

This publication of seventy-nine pages concludes with a bibliography and with a list of forty-one contemporary research studies dealing with aspects of architecture and the handicapped, some incomplete at the time the book went to press.

Designing for the Disabled (2nd edition, 1967) is a comprehensive, 207-page manual assembled by Selwyn Goldsmith. It is an almost incredibly complete and detailed catalogue of items of information about how to make everyday building elements, finishes, service installations, and general spaces so handicapped persons can use them. It is replete with illustrations, generally to scale. Although it does not focus on schools, it deals extensively with the more general topic of adapting public buildings for use by handicapped persons, and much of that section is applicable to schools.

The acting principle behind all of Goldsmith's suggestions and adjustments is that handicapped persons aspire to competence to manage their own affairs, and that every extra help they are given should be with that in mind. Rather than have an exclusive goal of personal normality, the handicapped individual is considered by this book to be aspiring toward personal maturity and toward contributing one's best in a complex society.

The emphasis is on accommodations for persons with sensory or other physical handicaps. Ways of adjusting for blindness, deafness, and various crippling conditions and other mobility-limiting conditions receive thorough treatment. Little in the book is applicable, except very indirectly, to mental retardation, maladjustment and mental illness, learning disabilities or speech handicaps.

Educational Change and Architectural Consequences is a report from Educational Facilities Laboratories written by Ronald Gross and Judith Murphy under the educational advisement of Robert Finley and Thomas R. Hasenphlug. Ronald W. Haase, an architect, was general director of the project. He designed the schematic architectural studies which were illustrated by Chapman, Goldsmith, and Yamasaki.

The central theme of the report is the flowering of individualized instruction in the United States and its impact on schools. After a forward, a chapter identifying the spirit of change, and another chapter on the instructional encounter, the authors move to concrete illustrations in building design.

The logistics of designing space which responds to the demand for individualization of instruction occupies the rest of the report. Sections are devoted to the preprimary school, the primary school, the middle school, and the secondary school.

Written in 1968, the report aptly selected and illustrated most of the ideas which were to receive acceptance by 1974. When this document is combined with the next one to be described, they form a solid descriptive base of the contemporary concepts for school facility design, whether for handicapped pupils, regular classes, or both combined.

A I A Journal, October, 1973. This issue of the official publication of the American Institute of Architects (1735 New York Avenue, N. W., Washington, D.C.) is entitled "A New Chapter in School Design." The introduction begins with this comment, "Change is apparent in our entire educational system. Possibly architects are more confronted with the immediate consequences of this than any other group. The shapes of our learning spaces are taking on new forms, forms that even today seem almost unorthodox to many."

The seven featured articles in the Journal, when studied in conjunction with the above *Educational Change and Architectural Consequences* supplies a substantial coverage of modern trends in educational design for all types of schools. The language of the articles, too, is readily understandable to persons who are not professional architects.

The Educational Management Review Series is a continuing series of surveys on educational topics prepared under the sponsorship of the Clearinghouse on Educational Management, a unit in the Educational Resources Information Center (ERIC). The latter is a national information system operated by the National Institute of Education, United States Department of Health, Education and Welfare.

The ERIC Clearinghouse on Educational Management, University of Oregon, Eugene, provides practicing educators with up-to-date reviews on significant topics. The following are recommended for careful study by all members of any team preparing to carry out the responsibility of designing space to be used by special education. Each runs from four to six pages and could, at this writing, be obtained free on request to the Clearinghouse.

Educational Management Review Series
"Year-Round Schools," S. C. Johnson, May 1972, No. 6.
"Class Size," I. Templeton, August 1972, No. 8.

"Differentiated Staffing," I. Templeton, September 1972, No. 9.
"Paraprofessionals," I. Templeton, November 1972, No. 11.
"School Size," I. Templeton, December 1972, No. 13.
"Nongraded Schools," W. Mellor, April 1973, No. 16.

Educational Facilities Review Series

"Open Plan Schools," A. A. Baas, July 1972, No. 6.
"Modular Components," A. A. Baas, July 1972, No. 7.
"Environments for the Physically Handicapped," A. A. Baas, August 1972, no. 8.
"Early Childhood Facilities," A. A. Baas, November 1972, No. 9.
"Relocatable Classrooms," A. A. Baas, January 1973, No. 10.
"Libraries and Instructional Materials Centers," A. A. Baas, February 1973, no. 13.
"Luminous Environments," A. A. Baas, March 1973, No. 15.
"Acoustical Environments," A. A. Baas, April 1973, No. 16.
"Thermal Environments," A. A. Baas, April 1973, No. 17.
"Site Selection," A. A. Baas, May 1973, No. 18.
"Site Development," A. A. Baas, July 1973, No. 19.
"Construction Management," A. A. Baas, September 1973, No. 20.

Our recommendation of the above management and facilities references is not to suggest that architects, school administrators, teachers, and board of education members are not aware of such matters. Rather, it is to help assure that all of the participants in planning and designing have ready access to the best of current thinking on those fast developing topics. Each of the above four- to six-page leaflets supplies not only an up-to-date summary of key material, but also an excellent bibliography for more detailed reference to any point one would wish to pursue further.

Organization of Sheltered Workshop Programs for the Mentally Retarded Adult, a 1971 book authored by J. L. Zaetz and published by Charles C Thomas, Springfield, is an excellent resource for concepts basic to designing sheltered workshops for the mentally retarded. These are growing rapidly in the United States, whether as parts of schools or as separate community installations. Public buildings originally erected for other purposes and still structurally sound are also being remodeled to make sheltered workshops. An excellent example is found in Butler, Pennsylvania, in what had been a Federal post office headquarters for the city.

Attention is called particularly to the first eight chapters in the Zaetz book. The approximately seventy pages devoted there to sheltered workshops organization and structure are quite useful.

Workshops for the Handicapped in the United States is a Charles C Thomas (Springfield) publication issued in 1971 and prepared by Nathan Nelson. This book is applicable to the design of sheltered workshop settings as well as for workshops which emphasize training for business or industrial placement of clients. Also, it concerns itself with the broad range of workshop populations: the blind, physically handicapped, those recovering from emotional or physical illness, and mixed populations. It does not contain recommendations regarding specifications, floor plans, or equipment. Rather, it provides the background out of which decisions about such matters can emerge.

We resisted the temptation to make the above list of basic references longer. It now contains six books, one journal issue, and eighteen leaflets. Altogether, the publications will occupy less than six inches of bookshelf space. Yet, we believe the package encompasses a solid core of background material of great potential help to those responsible for designing schools and schooling for the handicapped. A more extensive bibliography follows.

The following six organizations are well known for their constructive interest and concern for improving school architecture, facilities, and educational opportunities for all children including those who need special education. The names of key persons are included. It would be appropriate to direct inquiries to them to locate their most relevant recent material.

Dwayne E. Gardner, Executive Director
Council of Educational Facilities Planners International
29 W. Woodruff Avenue
Columbus, Ohio 43210

William C. Geer, Executive Director
The Council for Exceptional Children
1920 Association Drive
Reston, Virginia 22091

Edwin W. Martin, Associate Commissioner
Bureau for Education of the Handicapped
U.S. Office of Education
Washington, D.C. 20202

Laurence Molloy, Project Director
Educational Facilities Laboratories
477 Madison Avenue
New York, New York 10022

Maurice Payne, Director of Design Programs
The American Institute of Architects
1735 New York Avenue, N.W.
Washington, D.C. 20006

Beatrix Sebastian, Associate Secretary
American Association of School Administrators
1801 North Moore Avenue
Arlington, Virginia 22209

REFERENCES

1. Abel, Georgia Lee: Problems and trends in the education of blind children and youth. *Concerning the Education of Blind Children.* New York, American Foundations for the Blind, 1959.
2. Abeson, Alan, and Ackerman, Paul: *An Architectural-Educational Investigation of Education and Training Facilities for Exceptional Children,* Arlington, Council for Exceptional Children, 1965, p. 14.
3. Abeson, Alan: *The Design Process in Special Education Facility Planning,* Arlington, Council for Exceptional Children, Annual Convention, April, 1968, p. 7.
4. Abeson, Alan: *The Physical Environment: A Brave New World,* Arlington, Council for Exceptional Children, C.E.C. Selected Convention Papers, 1969, p. 13.
5. Abeson, Alan, and Berenson, Bertram: *Physical Environment and Special Education: An Interdisciplinary Approach to Research,* Arlington, Council for Exceptional Children, February, 1970, p. 33.
6. Abeson, Alan, and Blacklow, J.: *Environmental Design: New Relevance for Special Education,* Arlington, The Council for Exceptional Children, 1971.
7. Abramson, P.: *Schools for Early Childhood.* New York, Educational Facilities Laboratory, 1970.
8. Albee, F. H.: The effect of architectural barriers on the handicapped school child. *The Florida Architect, 14:27,* 1964.
9. Alberta plans new three million one-hundred-and-thirty thousand dollar hospital school. *Canadian Hospital, 42:45,* 1965.
10. *American Institute of Architects Workshop on Educational Facilities for Exceptional Children.* New York, Educational Facilities Lab., Inc., 1965, p. 94.
11. American Institute of Architects: A new chapter in school design. *AIA Journal,* October, 1973.
12. *American Standard Specifications for Making Buildings and Facilities Accessible to and Usable by the Physically Handicapped,* no. A117.1-1971, New York, American Standards Association, 1961.
13. Architectural Institute, Denver, Colorado: *Architectural Contributions to Effective Programming for the Mentally Retarded.* American Association of Mental Deficiency, 1967, p. 66.
14. Ashcroft, S. C.: Blind and partially seeing children. In Dunn, Lloyd M. (Ed.): *Exceptional Children in the Schools.* New York, HR&W, 1965.

15. Atterbury, D.: Rooms for wheel chair students. *Special Education, 56:*16-22, 1967.

16. Avery, Charlotte B.: The education of children with impaired hearing. In Cruickshank, W. M., and Johnson, G. O. (Eds.): *Education of Exceptional Children and Youth,* Englewood Cliffs, P-H, 1967.

17. Bair, H. V., and Leland, H.: *The Utilization and Design of Physical Facilities for the Rehabilitation of Mentally Retarded,* Parsons, Kansas, Parsons State Hospital & Training Center, 1957, p. 27.

18. Baker, Madeline, Fischetti, Michael A., and Young, Eddie M.: Where we stand on architecture barriers. *Rehabil. Rec., 9:*1, pp. 1-4, 1968.

19. Baumeister, A., and Butterfield, R. (Eds.): *Residential Facilities for the Mentally Retarded.* Chicago, Aldine, 1970.

20. Bayes, Kenneth: "The Therapeutic Effect of Environment on Emotionally Disturbed and Mentally Subnormal Children," London, A Kaufmann International Design Award Study, 1967, p. 58.

21. Bayes, K., and Francklin, S. (Eds.): *Designing for the Handicapped.* London, George Godwin Ltd., 1971, p. 79.

22. Bednar, M. J., and Haviland, D. S.: *The Role of the Physical Environment in the Education of Children with Learning Disabilities.* Rensselear Polytechnic Institute, Center for Architectural Research, New York, Educational Facilities Lab., Inc., March, 1969, p. 101.

23. Bender, Ruth E.: *The Conquest of Deafness.* Cleveland, Pr. of Case WR, 1970.

24. Benet, James, et al.: *The Project and the Schools.* New York, Educational Facilities Laboratories, 1967, p. 95.

25. Bereiter, C., and Engelmann, S.: *Teaching Disadvantaged Children in the Preschool.* Englewood Cliffs, P-H, 1966.

26. Berenson, Bertram: *Architecture for Exceptional Children,* Hampton, Hampton Institute, Division of Architecture, 1967, p. 7.

27. Berenson, Bertram: The planned environment: an educational tool. Council for Exceptional Children, *International Journal of Educational Science, 2:*123-125, 1968.

28. Birch, H. G.: *Brain Damage in Children.* Baltimore, Williams & Wilkins, 1964.

29. Birch, Jack W.: Estimating growth needs of special education in school districts. *Council of Administrators of Special Educators Newsletter, 11:*3. Pittsburgh, Stanwix, 1970, p. 4.

30. Birch, Jack W.: *Mainstreaming: Educable Mentally Retarded Children in Regular Classes,* Reston, Va., The Council for Exceptional Children, 1974, p. 104.

31. Birren, Faber: The emotional significance of color preference. *Am J Occup Ther, 6:*2, 1952, p. 5.

32. Bjannes, A. T., and Butler, E. W.: Environmental variation in community

care facilities for mentally retarded persons. *Am. J. Ment. Defic., 78*:4, pp. 429-39, 1947.

33. Boles, H. W.: Major considerations in the development of content and method of teaching school plant courses. In *Proceedings of Conference on the Role of School Administrators in the Planning, Development and Management of School Facilities.* Athens, University of Georgia, 1969, pp. 40-63.

34. Brenton, M.: Mainstreaming the handicapped. *Today's Education, March-April,* pp. 20-25, 1974.

34a. Brubeck, T., and Vanston, A. R.: Designing day care centers, *Ment. Retard., 12*:2, pp. 32-33, 1974.

35. Bryant, D. C.: Designing for the mentally handicapped. National Society for Crippled Children and Adults. *Rehabil. Lit., 25*:11, pp. 391-92, 1964.

36. Educational facilities for the visually handicapped, Microfilm, ED 028-617, Berkeley, Department of Architecture, California University.

37. Carter, John Harvey: Educational environment for the orthopedically handicapped, including the cerebral palsied. Sacramento, Bureau of Special Education, California State Department of Education, 1962.

38. Caudill, W.: What works and what fails in school design. *Nation's Schools, 79*:3, p. 32, 1967.

39. Christoflos, Florence, and Reng, Paul: A critical examination of special education programs. *Journal of Special Education,* Winter 3, pp. 371-79, 1969.

40. Colvin, R. W.: *The Design Process in Special Education Facility Planning Applied to a Day and Residential Facility for the Emotionally Disturbed and Brain Injured,* New York, Child Welfare League of America, 1968, p. 8.

40a. *Community/School: Sharing the Space and the Action.* New York, Educational Facilities Laboratories, Laurence Malloy, Project Director, 1973, p. 95.

41. Cook, D.: Program evaluation and review technique applications in education, in *U.S. Office of Education Cooperative Research Monograph, 17*:OE-12024, U.S. Government Printing Office, 1966.

42. *Cooperative School-Rehabilitation Centers,* Minneapolis, Educational Research and Development Council of the Twin Cities Metropolitan Area, Inc., University of Minnesota, 1970, p. 76.

43. Coot, Erwin, and Gautier, Manuel: *Center for Rehabilitation of Crippled Children.* Santo Domingo, Dominican Republic, Conescal #6, Mexico 10 D. F., 1967, p. 4.

44. Cruickshank, W. M., and Quay, H. C.: Learning and physical environment: the necessity for research and research design. *Exceptional Children,* December, pp. 261-68, 1970.

45. Dale, D. M.: Units for deaf children. London University Institute of Education, England. *Volta Review, 68:*7, pp. 496-99, 1966.
46. Daniels, A. S., and Davies, E. A.: *Adapted Physical Education: Principles and Practice of Physical Education for Exceptional Students,* 2nd ed., New York, Har-Row, 1965.
47. *General Survey and Brief History of the Development of Service Systems in Denmark,* Copenhagen, Danish National Service for the Mentally Retarded, 1969, p. 40.
48. DeAmbrosis, Clementina: Center for the Rehabilitation of Children. Sao Paulo, Brazil, Conescal #6, Mexico 10 D.F., 1967, p. 5.
49. Dembinski, R. J., and McCarthy, T. F.: Developmental disabilities: implementation and problems. *Ment. Retard., 12:*1, pp. 35-39, 1974.
50. *Design Criteria for Public School Plants Accommodating the Physical Disabled.* Jefferson City, School Building Services, Missouri State Department of Education, 1968, p. 5.
51. Designing instructional facilities for teaching the deaf: the learning module. In Symposium on Research and Utilization of Educational Media for Teaching the Deaf. *American Annals of the Deaf, 113:*5, 1968.
52. Drew, C. S.: Research on the psychological-behavioral effects of the physical environment. *Review of Educational Research, 41:*5, pp. 447-65, 1971.
53. Duner, K. (Ed.): *Guide to Construction of Social Welfare Facilities in Sweden During the 1960s.* Stockholm, National Association of Swedish Architects.
54. Dunn, Lloyd (Ed.): *Exceptional Children in the Schools.* New York, HR & W, 1965.
55. Dybwad, Gunnar: *Planning Facilities for Severely and Profoundly Retarded Adults.* New York, N.A.R.C. Reprint. 1969, p. 8.
56. *Planning and Development of Facilities for Preprimary Education,* Athens, Editorial Services, Department of Conferences, Bureau of Educational Studies and Field Services, University of Georgia, 1969, p. 82.
57. *Policies for Education in American Democracy,* Educational Policies Commission, National Education Association, 1946.
58. *Effect of Windowless Classrooms on Elementary School Children.* Ann Arbor Architectural Research Laboratory. New York, Educational Facilities Laboratories, Inc., 1965, p. 111.
59. Ellingson, Careth: *Directory of Facilities for the Learning-Disabled and Handicapped.* New York, Har-Row, 1972, p. 624.
59a. Engle, Rose C., and Gold, Beatrice: The early childhood unit—a lot of room for children to grow. *Teaching Exceptional Children, 6:*2, pp. 58-67, 1974.
60. Englehardt, N. L.: *Complete Guide for Planning New Schools.* West Nyack, Parker Publishing Company, Inc., 1970, p. 296.
61. *Design Needs of the Physically Handicapped: A Selected Bibliography,*

OEC-1-7-070883-5095, Madison, ERIC Clearinghouse on Educational Facilities, 1970, p. 38.

62. Etkes, Asher B., et al.: *Helping Rehabilitate the Handicapped Child through Successful Physical Play: A Symposium.* Long Island City, Playground Corporation of America, 1969.

63. *Exceptional Children in Regular Classrooms,* U.S. Office of Education, 1970, p. 78.

64. Fassler, J.: Performance of cerebral palsied children under conditions of reduced auditory input. *Except. Child.,* pp. 201-10, 1970.

65. Fassler, J., and Bryant, N. D.: Disturbed children under reduced auditory input: a pilot study. *Except. Child.,* November, pp. 179-204, 1971.

66. Fassler, J., and Bryant, N. D.: Teacher observations on using ear protectors for disturbed children. *Except. Child.,* November, pp. 254-56, 1971.

67. Fearn, D.: *Architectural Barrier Program of the National Society for Crippled Children and Adults,* Chicago, National Society for Crippled Children and Adults, 1966, p. 14.

68. Fitzroy, D., and Reid, J. L.: *Acoustical Environment of School Buildings.* New York, Educational Facilities Lab., Inc., 1963, p. 129.

69. Foote, Franklin M.: Classrooms for partially seeing children. *Except. Child., 22:1,* pp. 318-20, 1955.

70. Fowles, Beth: School buildings. In *Cerebral Palsy Review,* Cleveland, Highland View Hospital, January-February, 1961.

71. Frohreich, L. E.: Costing programs for exceptional children: dimensions and indices. *Except. Child.,* April, pp. 517-24, 1973.

72. Gabrielsen, M. A.: *Swimming Pools—A Guide to their Planning, Design, and their Operation.* Ft. Lauderdale, Hoffman Publications, Inc., 1969.

73. Gardner, D. E.: An ideal environment for learning, in *Housing for Early Childhood Education: Centers for Growing and Learning.* Bulletin 22-A, Washington, D.C., Association for Childhod Education International, 1968.

74. Garton, Malinda Dean: *Teaching the Educable Mentally Retarded— Practical Methods.* Springfield, Thomas, 1969.

75. Goforth, E. J.: *Suggestions and Guidelines for Development of Television Facilities in Schools for the Deaf,* Knoxville, Tennessee University, Southern Regional Media Center for the Deaf, 1968, p. 52.

76. Goldsmith, Selwyn: *Designing for the Disabled,* 2nd ed. New York, McGraw, 1967, p. 207.

77. Good, Carter F. (Ed.): *Dictionary of Education,* 2nd ed., New York, McGraw, 1969, p. 676.

78. Gordon, R.: The design of a preschool "learning laboratory" in a rehabilitation center, *Rehabilitation Monograph, 39,* New York, Institute of Rehabilitation Medicine, New York University Medical Center, 1969.

79. Gowan, J. C., and Demos, G. D.: *The Guidance of Exceptional Children.* New York, McKay, 1965.

80. Grant, G.: The handicapped university student. *Proc R Soc Med, 53,* pp. 1054-55, 1960.

81. Green, Allan C., and others: *Educational Facilities with New Media,* Troy, Rensselear Polytechnic Institute, Center for Architectural Research, 1966, p. 207.

82. Gross, R., and Murphy, J.: *Educational Change and Architectural Consequences.* New York, Educational Facilities Laboratory, 1968.

83. *Guide for Administrators Establishing Classrooms for Physically Handicapped Children,* Springfield, Illinois State Office of the Superintendent of Public Instruction, 1961.

84. *Handicapped Children Better Education,* Annual Report 575, U.S. Government Printing Office, 1968.

85. Haring, N. G., and Whelan, R. J.: *The Learning Environment: Relationship to Behavior Modification and Implications for Special Education,* vol. 16, no. 2, Lawrence, Kansas Studies in Education, School of Education, Kansas University, 1966, p. 68.

86. Hay, Louis, and Cohen, Shirley: Perspectives for a classroom for disturbed children. *Except. Child., 33:*8, 1967, pp. 577-80.

87. Hewett, F. M.: Educational engineering with emotionally disturbed children. California University, Los Angeles, Neuropsychiatric Institute. *Except. Child. 33:*7, 1967, pp. 459-67.

88. How to adapt a campus for students on wheels. *College Management, 2:*12, December, 1967, p. 27.

89. International Society for Rehabilitation of the Disabled: The physically disabled and their environment. Stockholm, *Stockholms Stads Arbetsvardsbyra,* 1961, 1972.

90. Johnson, Doris J., and Myklebust, Helmer R.: *Learning Disabilities.* New York, Grune, 1967.

91. Johnson, Warren E.: *Some Considerations in Designing Facilities for the Deaf,* Oregon, Portland Center for Hearing and Speech, 1967, p. 21.

92. Johnson, G. Orville: The education of mentally retarded children. In Cruickshank, William M., and Johnson, G. (Eds.): *Education of Exceptional Children and Youth,* 2nd ed. P-H, Englewood Cliffs, 1967.

93. Jones, J. W., and Collins, A. P.: *Educational Programs for Visually Handicapped Children,* bulletin 6, U.S. Government Printing Office, Office of Education, 1966.

94. Kahn, R. L.: The work module: a tonic for lunch pail lassitude. *Psychology Today,* February, pp. 35-39, 94, 1973.

95. *Some Organizational Considerations of Elementary Classrooms for Educable Mentally Retarded,* Topeka, Division of Special Education, Kansas State Department of Public Instruction, 1965, p. 12.

96. Kimbrell, D. L., et al.: Institutional environment developed for training severely and profoundly retarded. Abilene State School, Texas. *Ment. Retard., 5:*1, pp. 34-37, 1967.

97. King, Roy D.: *Patterns of Residential Care: Sociological Studies in Insti-*

tutions for Handicapped Children. London, Routledge & Kegan, 1971, p. 255.

98. Kirk, Samuel A.: *Educating Exceptional Children.* Boston, HM, 1972, p. 478.

99. Kirk, S. A., and Bateman, B.: Diagnosis and remediation of learning disabilities. *Except. Child., 29:2,* p. 73, 1962.

100. Kirk, S., and Johnson, G. O.: *Educating the Retarded Child.* Boston, HM, 1951.

101. Konig, Karl: The planning of residential schools for exceptional children. In Pietzner, Carlo Ed.): *Aspects of Curative Education.* Scotland, Aberdeen University Press, 1966, pp. 266-280.

102. Lance, W. D., and Kock, A. C.: Parents as teachers: self-help skills for young handicapped children. *Ment. Retard.,* June, pp. 3-4, 1973.

103. Lawson, Page: Play: a way to help realize the potential of sightless children. *Therapeutic Recreation Jurnal, III:*2nd qtr., 1969.

104. Lowenfeld, Berthold: *Our Blind Children,* 3rd ed., Springfield, Thomas, 1971.

105. Lowenfeld, B.: The child who is blind. *Journal of Exceptional Children, 19,* p. 96, 1952.

106. Mackie, Romaine P.: *Handicapped Children: School Housing,* bulletin 5.3-951/17, Office of Education, Federal Security Agency, 1952, p. 30.

107. Mackie, Romaine P.: *Special Education in the United States.* New York, Tchrs. Coll., 1969, p. 90.

108. Maeroff, Gene I.: Hope rises on education of handicapped students. *The New York Times,* April 21, p. 1, 1974.

109. *Making Facilities Accessible for the Physically Handicapped,* Lansing, act no. 1 of the Public Building Acts, Michigan State Legislature, 1966, p. 18.

110. *Making Facilities Accessible to the Physically Handicapped.* Albany, State U NY, 1967, p. 40.

111. Martin, William Edgar: Selected references on facilities and equipment for handicapped children, School Housing Section, Office of Education, U.S. Department of Health, Education and Welfare, 1963.

112. McCarthy, J. J., and McCarthy, J.: *Learning Disabilities.* Boston Allyn, 1969.

113. McMahan, Marie: *Educational Media Center: The Library's New Book,* Kalamazoo, Educational Resources Center, Western Michigan University, April, 1967, p. 29.

114. McQuade, Walter, and others: *Schoolhouse.* New York, Simon and Schuster, 1958.

115. Marrow, T. D., and Kohl, J. W.: Normative study of the administrative position in special education. *Except. Child.,* September, pp. 5-13, 1972.

116. Meecham, W. C.: Study summarized in education U.S.A., Arlington, National School Public Relations Association, October, 1972.

117. Milton, R., (Trans.): Care and education of exceptional children in

Finland, publication 23, Helsinki, Central Union for Child Welfare in Finland, 1963.

118. Moore, O. K.: Autolytic responsive environments and exceptional children. In Hellmuth, Jerome (Ed.): *Special Children in Century 21.* Seattle, Spec. Child, May, 1964.

119. Mullen, Frances A.: Chicago opens a new school for the physically handicapped. *Except. Child., 23:7*, pp. 296-299, 1957.

120. Nash, R. J., and Pfeffer, A.: *A Guide to a Special Class Program for Children with Learning Disabilities.* East Orange, New Jersey Association for Brain Injured Children, 1969.

121. Special education for handicapped children, in *First Annual Report,* National Advisory Committee on Handicapped Children, U.S. Office of Education, January, 1968.

122. *Standard Terminology for Curriculum and Instruction in Local and State School Systems,* OE-23052, U.S. Government Printing Office, National Center for Educational Statistics, 1970, p. 219.

123. National Education Association: *NEA Research Bulletin,* Washington, D.C., NEA, pp. 60-63, May, 1972.

124. NEA Research Bureau: Teacher opinion poll: involvement in school policy making. *Today's Education—NEA Journal,* February, pp. 11-12, 1973.

125. Neisworth, J. T., and Smith, R. M.: An analysis and redefinition of 'developmental disabilities'. *Except. Child.,* February, pp. 345-47, 1974.

126. Nellist, Ivan: *Planning Buildings for Handicapped Children.* Springfield, Thomas, 1970.

127. Nimmicht, G. P., and Partridge, A. R.: *Designs for Small High Schools,* Greeley, Educational Planning Service, Colorado State College, 1962.

128. Northcott, W. H. (Ed.): *The Hearing Impaired Child in a Regular Classroom: Preschool, Elementary and Secondary Years.* Washington, D.C., The Alexander Graham Bell Association for the Deaf, Inc., 1973, p. 301.

129. *Outdoor Recreation Planning for the Handicapped,* Bureau of Outdoor Recreation Technical Assistance Bulletin, Superintendent of Documents, 1967, p. 34.

130. Pate, John E.: Emotionally disturbed and socially maladjusted children. In Dunn, Lloyd M. (Ed.): *Exceptional Children in the Schools.* New York, HR & W, 1965.

131. *Places and Things for Experimental Schools.* New York, Educational Facilities Laboratory, Laurence Malloy, Project Director, 1972, p. 132.

132. Portland, Oregon, Board of Education, *Holladay Center for Handicapped Children,* Public Information Department, Portland Public Schools, Oregon 97206.

133. Probst, R., and Weinstock, R.: *High School: The Process and the Place.* New York, Educational Facilities Laboratory, 1972, p. 120.

134. Putnam, J. E., and Chismore, W. D.: *Standard Terminology for Curriculum and Instruction in Local and State School Systems,* State Education and Report Series I, Handbook VI, U.S. Government Printing Office, National Center for Educational Statistics, 1970.

135. *Design for All Americans. A Report of the National Committee on Architectural Barriers to Rehabilitation of the Handicapped.* U.S. Government Printing Office, Rehabilitation Services Administration, Superintendent of Documents, 1967.

136. Reissman, Frank: *The Culturally Deprived Child.* New York, Har-Row, 1962.

137. Salmon, F. C., and Salmon, C. F.: *Rehabilitation Center Planning.* University Park, Pa St U Pr, 1959.

138. Salmon, F. Cuthbert: *The Blind: Space Needs for Rehabilitation,* Stillwater, Office of Engineering Research, Oklahoma State University, 1964, p. 82.

139. Salmon, F. C., and Salmon, C. F.: *Sheltered Workshops: An Architectural Guide,* Stillwater, School of Architecture, Oklahoma State University, 1966, p. 124.

140. Schoenbohm, W. B.: *Planning and Operating Facilities for Crippled Children.* Springfield, Thomas, 1962, p. 311.

141. Scholl, G.: The education of children with visual impairments. In Cruickshank, William M., and Johnson, G. (Eds.): *Education of Exceptional Children and Youth,* 2nd ed. Englewood Cliffs, P-H, 1965.

142. *Schools and Playgrounds for Trainable Mentally Handicapped Children,* Ontario, Ontario Department of Education, 1971, p. 24.

143. Sebastian, B. (Ed.): School buildings 1973, in explanatory information to a filmstrip, American Association of School Administrators, 1973.

144. *Selected Abstracts—Physical Environment and Special Education,* Council for Exceptional Children, 1969, p. 22.

145. Shores, Richard E., and Haubrich, Paul A.: Effect of cubicles in educating emotionally disturbed children. *Except. Child., 36:1,* 1969.

146. Slotter, C. L.: Can open education fit in an egg crate?, in *Pennsylvania Education,* Harrisburg, Pennsylvania Department of Education, 1972, p. 2.

147. Small, Gloria: Environment and early education: an experimental course, Cleveland, Department of Education, Case Western Reserve University, 1793.

148. *Special Education Facilities for Emotionally Disturbed Children,* Ontario, Ontario Department of Education, p. 31.

149. Stevens, G. D.: Taxonomy in special education for children with body disorders, Pittsburgh, Department of Special Education and Rehabilitation, University of Pittsburgh, 1966.

150. Stevens, G. D., and Birch, J. W.: A proposal for clarification of the terminology used to describe brain injured children. *Except. Child., 23:8,* 1957.

151. Switzer, M. E.: Are colleges slighting the handicapped student? *Rehabil. Rec., 8,* pp. 1-4, 1967.
152. Taylor, W. W., and Taylor, J. W.: Special education of physically handicapped children in Western Europe. New York, International Society for the Welfare of Cripples, 1960.
153. Telford, Charles W., and Sawrey, James M.: The Exceptional Individual. Englewood Cliffs, P-H, 1967.
154. Tensone, S. L.: *Housing for Physically Handicapped, Guide for Planning and Designing.* 1968, p. 49.
155. *Architectural Considerations for Classrooms for Exceptional Children,* Austin, Division of Special Education, Texas Education Agency, 1967, p. 29.
156. *The Role of School in Rehabilitation Program,* in Proceedings of Gothenberg Seminar on Special Education, Lerum, Sweden, 1968, p. 92.
157. The Society and Home for Cripples in Denmark. Copenhagen, 1966, p. 60.
158. Trump, J. L. and Baynham, D.: *Focus on Change: Guide to Better Schools.* Chicago, Rand, 1961.
159. Tucker, W. V.: *Higher Education and Handicapped Students.* Emporia, Kansas State Teachers College, 1964.
160. *Mental Retardation Construction Program,* Secretaries Committee on Mental Retardation, U.S. Department of Health, Education & Welfare, 1969, p. 65.
161. Vanston, A. Rorke, et al.: *Design of Facilities for the Mentally Retarded: Diagnosis and Evaluation, Education and Training, Living Units,* Washington, D.C., Superintendent of Documents, 1965, p. 55.
162. Vanston, A. Rorke: A new deal in design for the mentally retarded. *Architectural Record. 141:2,* pp. 148-55, 1967.
163. Vellman, Ruth: A library for the handicapped. *School Library Journal, 13,* pp. 48-52, 1966.
164. Viscardi, Henry, Jr.: *School.* New York, Eriksson, 1964, p. 237.
165. Voss, D., et al.: Project design: deaf education. *Am Ann Deaf, 113,* pp. 1020-29, 1968.
165a. Waligura, Randolph L., et al.: *Environmental Criteria: M. R. Preschool Day Care Facilities,* Research Report, Social and Rehabilitation Services, Department of Health, Education and Welfare.
166. Watson, Thomas J.: *The Education of Hearing Handicapped Children.* Springfield, Thomas, 1967.
167. Wilson, Marguerite: Crippled and neurologically impaired children. In Dunn, Lloyd M. (Ed.): *Exceptional Children in the Schools.* New York, HR & W, 1965.
168. Witengier, M.: An adaptive playground for physically disabled children with perceptual deficits: the Magruder environmental therapy complex, Orlando, Orange County Board of Public Instruction.
169. Wolf, J. M.: Physical facilities guidelines for handicapped children, fitting facilities to the child. *School Management, 11:2,* pp. 40-54, 1967.

170. Wolf, J. M.: *Physical Facilities for Exceptional Children in the Schools,* Balboa, Design Specialty.

171. Wooden, H. Z.: Deaf and hard of hearing children. In Dunn, Lloyd M. (Ed.): *Exceptional Children in the Schools.* New York, HR & W, Albertson, New York, Human Resources Center, 1968, p. 53.

172. Yuker, H. E., et al.: *Design of a School for Physically Disabled Students,* 1965.

INDEX